THE PAIN A

GW01418757

Also by the Same Author

CONFIRM YOUR FAITH

The Pain and the Glory

A Journey in Israel through the Rosary

WILLIAM WESTON

**with a Foreword by
the Bishop of Lewes**

The Canterbury Press
Norwich

Copyright © William Weston 1987, 1990

First published 1990 in this revised edition by
The Canterbury Press Norwich
(a publishing imprint of Hymns Ancient & Modern Limited)
St Mary's Works, St Mary's Plain,
Norwich, Norfolk, NR3 3BH

Previously published 1987 by St John's Publishing Group
Gordon, N.S.W. Australia.

British Library Cataloguing in Publication Data
Weston, William
The pain and the glory.-Rev.ed.
1. Christian life. Prayer. Rosary
I. Title
242.74

ISBN 1-85311-020-5

Typeset by Cambridge Composing UK Limited
and printed in Great Britain by
St Edmundsbury Press, Suffolk

For the Order of St Lazarus of Jerusalem

The Order of St Lazarus is a military and hospitaller order of chivalry. It was founded in the twelfth century on an ancient monastic order dedicated to the care of lepers. Today throughout the world the Order is pledged to foster Christian Unity and work for the benefit of suffering humanity.

Foreword

St John of the Cross said that the Rosary was like throwing a bone to the dog, so that the 'pray-er' could cross safely over the road. Here is a way in which the mind can be brought into submission, whilst the heart is lifted by grace to God. In 'The Pain and the Glory' this beautiful lifting is described in a way which allows the heart almost to be propelled into glory. For the mysteries are set in the land where He who took me into glory through his incarnation, Passion and Resurrection, lived and loved. The mysteries are set in the poetry of him, who took upon himself the form of a servant, and also the lovely place of Mary in this work is set out without sentimentality or intrusion as the main Person.

The primary reason that we pray is simply to give God time to love us. The mysteries of the Rosary are part of that love which God pours on us. They are the way in which He shows his love. This book will help to make that love real; that love to be seen to be a part of the visible world; and still to be shown now, as it was once poured on us in the earthly life of Jesus Christ.

Fr. Bill Weston has made mystery part of our life without diminishing the glory. I hope this book will be much used.

Peter Lewes

Contents

ACKNOWLEDGEMENTS

The author expresses his gratitude to Cassell Plc for a quotation from *Simeon's Song* by Father Andrew S.D.C. (Mowbray imprint), also for ideas from Canon Frank Colquhoun in *Preaching through the Christian Year 2* (Mowbray imprint), and also for Laurence Housiman (1865–1959), from *The English Hymnal*; to Rich & Cowan Ltd, publishers, for information from *In the Steps of the Master* by H.V. Morton; to S.C.M Press Ltd, publishers, for quotations from *Crucified and Crowned* by William Barclay; to Collins Plc for quotations from *Naught for your Comfort* by Trevor Huddleston; to the Bible Society for use of biblical texts; to the Rt Revd Peter Ball, Bishop of Lewes, for writing the Foreword; to the Revd Gilbert Sinden S.S.M. previously of St George's College Jerusalem for his description of the Orthodox Easter in the Church of the Holy Sepulchre; to the Rt Revd Kalistos Ware of the Greek Orthodox Church in England, for extracts from a sermon preached in Christ Church Cathedral, Oxford; to Mr Keith Ellis for the cover photograph of a stained glass window in St Martin's Parish Church, West Drayton, Middlesex.

THE PAIN AND THE GLORY

CHAPTER ONE

Approaching the Mysteries

Follow now the Gospel story.
Read the Word of God again.
Those who hope to share the glory
Must be prepared to share the pain.

'I am sorry we have to treat you like this,' said the bright young Israeli security officer, 'but there is great danger here and everyone has to be protected.'

I was preparing to board the aircraft at Tel Aviv airport to return to London after my pilgrimage to the Holy Land.

Very carefully my luggage was examined.

Only a few weeks before, a plastic bomb had been discovered in a false base of a very ordinary travelling bag. It would have blown up the plane had not one of these very perceptive and highly trained young officials detected it.

'Thank you,' said the young man taking my passport and comparing the photograph with the person standing in front of him.

'Now I must ask you some questions.'

Obviously he had been trained well in this procedure.

1

'When did you come to Israel? Why did you come? Whom did you meet? Where did you go? Did anyone you met introduce you to anyone else? Did anyone speak to you at the airport? Where did those you met in Israel live? What nationality were they? Where did you stay?' and so on and on he went, always most courteous, coming back to one or other of the questions if there was any faltering on my part, throwing in a few trick questions that might catch anyone off guard who had an ulterior motive.

At last he returned my passport.

'I hope you will come back to Israel again. Have a good trip home,' he said.

What did I do in Israel? What was the purpose of my visit? Where did I go?

Some of the answers to these questions will be provided in the following pages.

*   *   *

My room at the hotel in Tel Aviv was on the eighteenth floor. It had a small balcony overlooking a row of flat beaches. These beaches were separated from several large hotels by a promenade. The beaches stretched south to a headland a few miles away on which stood the ancient town of Jaffa, known once as Joppa.

Tel Aviv is the largest city in Israel. It has grown into a vast mass of concrete buildings since it was founded in 1901 on desolate sand dunes on the eastern shore of the Mediterranean Sea.

It was the Jewish New Year, *Rosh Hashannah*, and everyone was in a holiday mood. The beaches were crowded and the hotels were full of families. Hundreds of sail board riders glided on the smooth sea, weaving their colourful craft around the groups of stone breakwaters which had been built at intervals about a hundred yards from the shore.

That evening at sunset, hundreds and hundreds of people gathered along the promenade and faced the setting sun which was eventually swallowed by the purple sea, lighting the western sky in a blaze of crimson glory.

Many of the people were very well dressed. The children wore white and all the males had their heads covered. They all had prayer books. Some prayed alone, others stood and prayed together in groups.

They were praying for the forgiveness of their sins, which they believed would depart from them like the setting sun, and so begin the new year at peace with God.

Next day, with the party I had joined, we went to Jaffa, which in ancient times was the seaport to Jerusalem.

Jaffa stands as a witness to God's universal dominion. It was from Jaffa that Jonah sailed, in his attempt to flee from the task which God had called him to do, to urge the sinful Gentiles of Ninevah to repent.

It was in Jaffa that Peter was called to preach the Gospel of Jesus Christ to the Gentile Roman, Centurion Cornelius and his household, and so begin the proclamation of the Gospel to all the world.

There is a fountain in the form of a whale in Jaffa,

a reminder of the ultimate success of Jonah's mission. There is also a large church called St Peter's, which gives its testimony of the fulfilment of the prophecy that Christ is to be a light to the Gentiles as well as to be the glory of his people Israel.

Here is actually the purpose of this book, to proclaim the light and glory bestowed on us through the pain and passion of Jesus Christ.

Later we shall see the Blessed Virgin Mary presenting her forty days old baby in the temple at Jerusalem, and old Simeon prophesying that her child was to be a light to lighten the Gentiles as well as the glory of Israel, telling Mary that a sword of pain would pierce her own soul.

We shall see how the light came into the world through Mary's obedience, how the sword pierced her soul through the suffering of her son and how his glory was given to her and to all who would become members of the new Israel, the Christian Church.

We left Jaffa and followed the way of St Peter along the Plain of Sharon to Caesarea, where Peter preached to, and baptised the Roman garrison centurion, Cornelius and all who were in his home.

Later St Paul, in the midst of bitter hostility from Jews, also admitted Gentiles into the Church.

At Caesarea, St Paul gave his testimony of the power of the risen Christ. After two years imprisonment there, he was summoned before King Agrippa to whom he spoke about his own conversion and the resurrection of Jesus Christ. From Caesarea, Paul was taken to Rome where, from his prison he wrote letters to the Gentile churches at Colossae, Philippi and Ephesus, showing

Jesus Christ indeed as a light to the Gentiles and the glory of Israel.

The actions of Peter and Paul, in baptising Gentiles, were ratified at *The Council of Jerusalem*. It was then that Christianity became a universal religion (Acts 15).

Unlike Jaffa, Caesarea, once the luxurious dwelling place of King Herod and Pontius Pilate, is now a ruin. In 1956 archaeologists made a rare find, a stone bearing the inscription of Pontius Pilate. All that remains of Caesarea now are, a Roman water duct, a Roman theatre, some stables and a few other buildings including fortifications of the Crusaders.

Hundreds of tourists were at Caesarea. We sat on the tiered stone seats of the ancient semi circular theatre. A girl stood on the stage and sang *Amazing Grace*, demonstrating not only the quality of her voice, but also the skill of those ancient builders in acoustic engineering. Every word could be clearly heard.

From Caesarea we went on to Acre, stopping on Mount Carmel to look down on Haifa, Israel's largest sea port.

Acre was called Ptolemais when St Paul stayed there for a day to encourage the followers of Christ, when he was on his way to Caesarea and Jerusalem at the end of his third missionary journey (Acts 21.7).

Acre was to be the scene of glory and defeat in another milenium, as the last bastion of the Crusaders in the Holy Land.

The remnant of the gigantic stone fortress which was built by the Crusaders, still proclaims their resourcefulness.

Richard the Lion Heart recaptured Acre in 1191

after it had fallen into Moslem hands and, for the next one hundred years the Crusaders held out, often against overwhelming odds in the thick walled castle, bounded on three sides by a wide moat, and by the Mediterranean Sea on the fourth. Its fall in 1291 marked the end of the Crusades.

4   The great stone fortress is now being restored. Rooms, large and small within the building are linked by a maze of passages, some low and damp. It was necessary for us to stoop as we walked through these narrow, seeping defilements. The Knights of St John and St Lazarus had crawled along them in their endurance of bitter suffering, even to death.

My mind went back to the Conference of *The Order of St Lazarus* which I had attended a few weeks before at Oxford, where five hundred successors of those knights of St Lazarus had gathered to rededicate themselves to the ideals for which the knights at Acre had died in that ancient citadel.

During the Oxford conference, on a golden autumn day, we were taken to *Stonor Park* near Henley, the home of an English noble family, where battles for religious freedom had been fought during the Reformation period.

At *Stonor Park* we witnessed a fascinating display of the weapons and armoury used by the knights during the time of the Crusades.

On lustrous grass which sloped up through scattered trees to meet a cloudless, blue sky, armour clad men went through the actions of armed combat with swords, staves, javelins and arrows. Others riding horses adorned with colourful caparisons, charged at each other to bring their opponents to the ground with lances. The combatants were watched by their ladies, elegantly dressed in long tight waisted gowns and high pointed hats.

The display area on which the jousting, duelling and archery took place was surrounded by striped pavilions, some red and white, some blue and white, flying long triangular, coloured pennons from their centre poles.

It all seemed so fanciful and enchanting, quite remote from the stark, stone battlements of the Crusaders' fortress at Acre, at the end of the arid brown terrain where the entire contingent of the hospitaller knights of St Lazarus died, ministering to the needs of others.

Leaving Acre we went inland to Nazareth where on behalf of all humanity, the Blessed Virgin Mary accepted her vocation to be the Mother of God in human flesh.

In this book I hope to show the Mother of Jesus as a source of unity through the example of her complete obedience, seeking nothing for herself, except the fulfilment of God's will.

I propose to do this, using the fifteen mysteries of the Rosary as signs of the love and purpose of God wrought in Christ for each one of us.

Many people are under the impression that the Rosary is an act of worship directed to the Blessed Virgin Mary. It is not. The Rosary is actually a series of meditations on the text –

'God so loved the world that he gave his only begotten Son, that whoever believes in him shall not perish, but have everlasting life' (John 3.16).

The operative word is *gave*. God *gave* his Son.

The meditations of the Rosary are focused on how God gave, the cost of the giving and the benefit of the gift.

The part of Mary in the mysteries is as the representative of us all, as a human being who responded in absolute obedience to the will of God.

It was through her that God gave his Son to the world to share completely the life of humanity.

We are in good company in honouring Mary. The angel Gabriel told her that she was highly favoured by God. St Luke tells us that it was the Holy Spirit who enabled her cousin Elizabeth to echo the angel's greeting and declare that she was blessed among women.

We are not taught to pray to Mary. Christian people can only pray to the Father in the power of the Holy Spirit, in the name of, or through, our Saviour Jesus Christ who is also our Lord.

We worship the God of the living. Therefore, just as we may ask for the prayers of any follower of Christ in this life, we can surely ask to be included in the prayers of Mary whom Christ himself commended to us, through his disciple St John, to be John's mother and ours.

In my book *The Glory of the Word*, I have stated that John described himself as *the disciple whom Jesus loved*, because he wanted his readers to see him as the personification of themselves. Therefore, when our Lord commended his mother to *the disciple whom he loved*, he was commending her to us all, because each of us is *the disciple he loves*.

To God alone we pray for forgiveness, for guidance and strength.

All we ask from Mary, is what we might ask from any devout lover of God whose faith has inspired us, that she pray for us on our pilgrimage in this life.

       *   *   *

The great events which are the subjects of meditation in the Rosary are called mysteries.

A mystery is something hidden, a great wonder to be revealed.

The mysteries of the Kingdom of God have been revealed through Jesus Christ. The mysteries which form the subjects of the meditations of the Rosary include the revelation of God's love for man, described in the last of the psalms as 'his noble acts and his excellent greatness.'

The Rosary is divided into three sections. These are, the five joyful mysteries, the five sorrowful mysteries and the five glorious mysteries.

The five joyful mysteries are; the Annunciation by the angel Gabriel to Mary that she had been highly favoured and called by God to be the mother of the long promised Messiah; the Visitation by Mary to her cousin Elizabeth who, filled with the Holy Spirit, confirmed the message of the angel; the Birth of Jesus in Bethlehem; the Presentation of Jesus at the purification of Mary; the Finding of Jesus at the age of twelve in the temple, after he had been lost for three days during a visit to Jerusalem.

In these events the Blessed Virgin Mary was active. She was the subject, the doer.

Mary responded to the message of the angel; Mary visited Elizabeth; Mary gave birth to Jesus; Mary presented Jesus in the temple at her purification; Mary found the twelve year old Jesus in the temple.

The five sorrowful mysteries are, the Agony of Jesus in the Garden of Gethsemane, the Scourging of Jesus, the Crowning of Jesus with thorns, Jesus bearing the Cross and the Crucifixion of Jesus.

In these, Mary was completely passive.

She had no control over the terrible events. She was a grief stricken witness.

The five glorious mysteries are, the Resurrection, the Ascension, the Outpouring of the Holy Spirit at Pentecost, the Assumption of the Blessed Virgin Mary from this world into Heaven and her Coronation in Heaven.

In these Mary was the forerunner of all mankind. She was the recipient of the acts of God in the resurrection of her Son from the dead and his ascension into Heaven.

Mary waited with the company of believers for the outpouring of the Holy Spirit at Pentecost and saw the beginning of the Church her Son had promised to build in the world.

When life in this world was over, because of the death and resurrection of her Son, Mary went to the place in the heavenly mansions of the Father which her Son had prepared for her. A similar place he has promised to us.

There she received the crown promised to all who

believe in her son and have striven to fulfil his will (2 Timothy 4.8; Revelation 2.10).

The Rosary may be accompanied by manual acts using special beads. The word *bead* originally meant a prayer.

The purpose of Rosary beads is to help to keep the mind of the person meditating fixed on the mysteries which unfold God's love for us in giving his son Jesus Christ, that we may have everlasting life.

The use of a counting aid to assist prayers, or beads, is not confined to Christianity.

The origin of the Rosary beads in the Christian Church has been attributed to St Dominic, the founder of the great preaching order in the twelfth century, which still bears his name, *The Dominicans*.

The theme of Dominic's preaching was concentrated on the fifteen mysteries of the Rosary, and the purpose of the beads was to enable the people, many of whom then were illiterate, to remember the mysteries.

At the time, a heresy which began in a town called Albi in Provence, France, was attracting many people. Those who succumbed to the heresy were called Albigenses. They believed that the soul was imprisoned in the body and that all material things belonged to Satan.

The pious tradition of the origin of the Rosary is that the Blessed Virgin Mary appeared to Dominic when he was combating this heresy. It is said that she gave him a Rosary promising him success in his mission if he would preach its mysteries.

Rosary beads are used to assist the meditations of the heart and mind by manual actions.

The Rosary takes its name from a rose garden,

which the Dominicans found condusive to meditation, using the beads to assist their meditations.

The Rosary is made up of a pendant which consists of a cross or crucifix, a large bead, three small beads and another large bead attached by a medallion, to a circle of five groups of ten small beads separated by five large beads.

As the cross is held in the hands, *The Apostles' Creed* is said. The fingers move to the first large bead and *The Lord's Prayer* is said. As each of the three small beads passes through the fingers a **Hail Mary* is said. Then follows the saying of 'Glory to the Father and to the Son and to the Holy Spirit as in the beginning so now and forever, Amen', as the next large bead is held.

While holding the medallion *The Lord's Prayer* is said to begin the meditation of the first of either the joyful, sorrowful or glorious mysteries.

The mystery is contemplated as a *Hail Mary* is said ten times while the ten small beads pass through the fingers, followed by the saying of *Glory to the Father* etc. as the large bead is held. This process follows for the rest of the meditation. Each section is introduced by *The Lord's Prayer* and concludes with *Glory to the Father*, etc – both said while the large beads are held.

There are those who say that this form of meditation was condemned by our Lord in the Sermon on the Mount when he said 'When you pray do not use vain repetitions' (Matthew 6.7). He then went on to teach his own prayer saying, when you pray, pray like this – 'Our Father . . .' (Matthew 6.9).

* For an explanation of the *Hail Mary* see page 23.)

Possibly there is no prayer which has become a vain repitition more often than *The Lord's Prayer*. A moment's reflection on the way most of us have said it at some time will convince us of this. Our Lord derided the use of vain repetitions, not devotional repetitions which are frequent in scripture. Any prayer can become a vain repetition, a purposeless repetition and this is exactly what the saying of the devotions of the Rosary is intended to avoid.

Psychologists teach about the power of auto suggestion by the use of words repeated to influence the mind.

The devotions of the Rosary are intended to help those who use them to keep their minds on the subject of their meditation, as they pray the *Our Father*, taught by Christ himself, state the words of scripture which emphasise God's plan for man's salvation through the obedience of Mary, reminding themselves of the wider fellowship of the blessed ones as they ask the Mother of God incarnate to pray with them and for them.

Often in worship, those present are bidden to pray for each other. The apostle James wrote, 'pray for each other that you may be made whole' (James 5.16).

If we can request the prayers of those who worship with us on earth, is it not natural that, being aware of our union with the cloud of those who witness to us of their faith (Hebrews 12.1), we should ask her, the example of human obedience and devotion to God's will, to pray for us?

CHAPTER TWO

Prophecies of the Pain

(The Joyful Mysteries)

The first of the Joyful Mysteries is the Annunciation.

For this how wondrously he wrought!
A maiden, in her lowly place,
Became in ways beyond all thought,
The chosen vessel of his grace.

She bowed her to the Angel's word
Declaring what the Father willed,
And suddenly the promised Lord
That pure and hallowed temple filled.

Gabriel, the messenger from God came to Mary of Nazareth and announced to her that she had been called to be the Mother of the long promised Saviour.

When the messenger from God came to Mary in Nazareth, the township was quite small. Today Nazareth is a large town. We arrived there about 4 p.m. And descended through the busy traffic infested main road, across which people of many races were walking in all directions. Our coach was parked and we joined the bustling crowds, weaving past beggars and sellers of

15

postcards and souvenirs, to *The Church of the Annunciation*.

Nazareth seemed to be a very dirty place. In the main street a vacant block between two shops was actually covered with discarded plastic bags and other rubbish. The streets also were full of litter. Flies buzzed around open fruit shops in which men with grubby hands were crushing pomegranates and offering the juice to passers by for half a shekel a glass.

Joseph's shop would have been open to the thoroughfare and the family would have lived within its walls.

The Church of the Annunciation is the great gem of Nazareth. The pale golden building was completed in 1968. It replaced the last of several churches which had stood on the site, identified as the place where the Angel of the Lord came to Mary.

I was glad that we visited Nazareth before we had been to Bethlehem and Jerusalem, because the Incarnation began in Nazareth when Mary responded to the call of God.

'Hail Mary, you are highly favoured, the Lord is with you. Fear not you have found favour with God – you will conceive and bear a son and you will name him Jesus. He shall be great and be called the Son of the Highest. He shall be given the throne of David and shall reign over the house of Jacob for ever – there will be no end of his kingdom.'

And Mary asked, 'How shall this be?'

The reply was the reply which is given to each one of us when God gives us a special task. Often we may face a duty which seems impossible to fulfil, just as Mary felt at the Annunciation – How can I do this? – and the answer from God's messenger is the answer given to us all.

'The Holy Spirit will come upon you and the power of the Highest will overshadow you.'

Mary responded in complete obedience, 'Behold, I am the handmaid of the Lord, let it be to me, according to your word' (Luke 1.26–38).

The Church of the Annunciation in Nazareth is both a testimony to Mary's obedience and also to the universality of the humanity which was the fruit of it. The octagonal tower seen from the road which descends into Nazareth dominates the town. Inside the building as one looks up from beneath the tower, it is seen as the representation of a white lily rooted in Heaven, opening towards the place where it is believed Mary accepted her vocation. The petals of the flower are gleaming white and their edges, joined to form a sixteen pointed star also form a recurring M for Mary.

The universality of the Son of Mary is seen in the gifts from all over the world with which the church has been adorned. Many of these gifts, in the form of paintings, mosaics and windows identify Mary and her son with the people of the countries from which the gifts have come. So there are to be seen black Madonnas, and white Madonnas, yellow Madonnas and brown Madonnas.

We were taken over *The Church of the Annunciation* by an old Arab guide. He wore a shabby grey suit with a collar and tie. His head was covered with a rather dirty head cloth. I think he was a Moslem, however, as he identified each part of the church, he spoke as if he had actually been present when Joseph was a carpenter in Nazareth. His advice to the ladies was – 'try to be happy and you will stay beautiful and live longer.'

*   *   *

The second joyful mystery is the Visitation of Mary, to her cousin Elizabeth.

> *'Whence,' she cried, at that fair meeting,*
> *'Comes to me this great reward?*
> *For when first I heard the greeting*
> *Of the Mother of my Lord,*
> *In my womb, the joy repeating,*
> *Leapt my babe in sweet accord!'*

When the messenger from God announced to Mary that she had been chosen to be the mother of the Messiah, he also told her that her aged cousin Elizabeth was to have a child.

Luke tells us that Mary visited her cousin Elizabeth, who was to be the mother of John the Baptist. This would have involved a journey through arid, dangerous country of about sixty miles.

Matthew does not mention the visit of Mary to Elizabeth, but he does say that when Joseph learned that Mary was going to have a baby, not willing to make her a public example, he decided to put her away privately.

Some writers have suggested that, prior to Mary's engagement to Joseph, her parents had both died and that she had lived with Elizabeth until she was old enough to go to Nazareth to prepare for her marriage to Joseph.

If this were so, *to put her away privately* could have meant sending her back to Elizabeth as soon as possible. Elizabeth knew that the child Mary was to bear was to be the long promised Messiah.

The revelation of the identity of Mary's child to Joseph could have been made while Mary was with Elizabeth. Elizabeth may have confirmed the dream of Joseph with a letter, urging him to take Mary back.

The traditional birth place of John the Baptist is Ain Karin. There is no mention of this in the Bible, but the tradition is very strong. I saw a beautiful Franciscan church commemorating the birth of John in that village which lies in a valley surrounded by hills, a few miles on the western side of Jerusalem.

However, when Mary visited her kinswoman Elizabeth, St Luke wrote that she went into the hill country with haste, to a city, Judah and entered into the house of Zacharias and greeted Elizabeth (Luke 1.39).

When this passage was translated into English, the preposition *of* was added before Judah, thus giving the impression that Mary went to a city in the region of Judea. However, in the original Greek there is no preposition before *Iouda* which Greek lexicons agree is an indeclinable word. The Greek word *Iouda* is used both for the region of Judah and for the town Juttah, which was one of twelve towns around Hebron given by Joshua to the priests. As a priest, it is likely that Zacharias would have lived there with Elizabeth.

After Joshua had conquered Palestine, the heads of the priestly tribe, the Levites, came to Eleazar and

Joshua with the elders of Israel saying, 'The Lord commanded by the hand of Moses to give us cities to dwell in and land for our cattle' (Joshua 21.1–2).

So they gave them Hebron in the hill country of Judah, and twelve other places in the surrounding area, including Juttah, for the descendants of Aaron, the priests (Joshua 26.13, 16, 19).

If John the Baptist was born in Ain Karin, Elizabeth would possibly have left Juttah shortly before his birth.

Nothing is known of how Mary made that long and difficult journey of about sixty miles over very desolate country. At that time there were no roads, merely trade routes. It would have been necessary for her to join a group of travellers going that way, for she could not have gone alone to the Hebron region from Nazareth.

It is amazing how many incidents recorded in the Scriptures have prophetic significance.

The sun rises on Jerusalem over the Mount of Olives.

Sunrises and sunsets in the Holy Land have a special unique beauty. I saw the sun rise on several occasions while I was in Israel. We were always up early and wanted to make the most of every day. One morning, while I was swimming in the Sea of Galilee near Tiberias, I saw the sun rise like a ball of fire over the Golan Heights. On another occasion I saw the sun rise while I was bobbing about like a cork in the buoyant waters of the Dead Sea. There, it peered through the haze which lay over the white limestone walls of the Plain of Moab.

However, nothing can be compared with the sun rising over the Mount of Olives, casting its rays on Jerusalem.

Away to the South West is Hebron, then the highest town in Judea, where King David united all the tribes.

In the days when Mary visited Elizabeth in the Hebron region, the gates of the temple in Jerusalem were opened at sunrise, and the first sacrifice was offered.

H. V. Morton describes the following in *In The Steps of the Master*.

Every morning just before dawn, a priest stood on one of the towers of the temple, while the other priests on duty for the day, assembled below.

As the sun rose, the priest on the tower chanted, 'The sun shineth already.' Those below responded, 'Is the sky lit up as far as Hebron?'

Then, when the rays of the morning sun had reached the hill country, and the distant town of Hebron was bathed in its light, the priest on the tower sang, 'It is lit up as far as Hebron.'

Immediately the silver trumpets would sound, the gates of the temple would be flung open and the first morning sacrifice would be offered.

Day by day this happened, until the temple was destroyed in A.D. 70.

Perhaps the prophet Malachi, whose book is the last in *The Old Testament* had the morning sacrifice in his mind when he foretold the coming of the Messiah saying 'To you who fear the Lord will the Sun of Righteousness rise with healing his wings.'

When Mary came to the home of Zacharias and Elizabeth in the Hebron region, Elizabeth was filled with the Holy Spirit and, through the Holy Spirit's enlightenment, (the spirit of knowledge) she was enabled to recognise her young cousin as the mother of the Messiah.

As the rays of the rising sun reached Hebron every morning, the first sacrifice of the day was offered in the temple at Jerusalem.

So when Mary came to that region, with the Word of God taking humanity in her womb, Elizabeth knew that the light of the Sun of Righteousness was already shining there and that the great sacrifice for the world was ready to begin.

'Whence is this that the mother of my Lord should come to me,' greeted Elizabeth. 'Blessed are you among women, and blessed is the fruit of your womb.'

The greeting of Elizabeth was confirmation for Mary of the message of the angel. The ageing Elizabeth was, as the angel had said, six months pregnant. The baby growing in her womb to be the herald of the Messiah, made his first proclamation of the Messiah by leaping in his mother's womb.

Mary sang her praise to God in the canticle called *The Magnificat*.

'My soul magnifies the Lord, and my spirit rejoices in God my Saviour,

for he has regarded the low estate of his handmaiden,

For behold, henceforth, all generations will call me blessed.'

When Mary proclaimed that all generations would call her *blessed*, she was making her own acceptance of the salutation of Elizabeth and of the angel, who both said that she was blessed among women.

The word *blessed* means *set apart for God's purpose* and Mary acknowledged her unique and wonderful vocation. Therefore the Bible decrees that she should always be called Blessed Mary, or Holy Mary.

In the act of devotion beginning *Hail Mary* which is used daily by millions of Christians, both the Annunciation and the Visitation are recalled by the words of Gabriel, 'Hail Mary, full of grace, the Lord is with thee' (Luke 1.28), and also by the words of Mary's cousin Elizabeth, 'Blessed art thou among women and blessed is the fruit of thy womb, Jesus' (Luke 1.42). (The Greek word *kecharitomene* has been translated as *highly favoured* and *full of grace* from Latin.)

Then, rejoicing in the Communion of Saints, the fellowship of that blessed company of all faithful people who surround us to bear witness to us of their faith (Hebrews 12.1) the simple request is made, 'Holy Mary, Mother of God, pray for us sinners now and at the hour of our death.'

Such a request we could make to anyone in this world or the next who has earned the right to be called blessed.

Mary was the Mother of God because the child she brought into the world was the Word of God. Through Mary's obedience the Word was made flesh and dwelt amongst us. The Word who *was* in the beginning, was God and is God, and he was born of the Virgin Mary.

*　　　*　　　*

The third joyful mystery is the Incarnation, the birth of Jesus.

> *He shrank not from the oxen's stall,*
> *He lay within the manger bed,*
> *And He Whose bounty feedeth all,*
> *At Mary's breast Himself was fed.*

Mary stayed with Elizabeth for three months. Then she returned to Nazareth and married Joseph who had been told the true identity of the child Mary was to bear.

The journey back to Nazareth would have been much harder for her because, by now she was three or four months with child.

We can imagine the care Elizabeth would have taken to ensure that her young kinswoman, whom she knew was to be the Mother of her Lord, would have the safest and easiest journey to Nazareth.

We can also imagine the joy and eagerness with which Joseph would have received her in Nazareth as his wife.

Only a few months after Mary's return to Nazareth came the decree of the Emperor, requiring every man to return to the place of his birth to be registered. This made it necessary for Joseph to take Mary back on that southern route to Jerusalem and on to Bethlehem.

The Kingdom of Judah, of the line of David had ceased to exist since the devastation of Jerusalem and its temple by the Babylonians in 586 B.C. but all through the years the record of the line had been kept.

In both *The Old Testament* and *The New Testament* there is abounding evidence of the importance the Jews placed on lineage and ancestry. Both Matthew and

Luke point to Joseph as the living successor of King David; Matthew through the royal line and Luke through the natural line.

This means that, had the kingdom still existed, Joseph of Nazareth would have been King of Judah.

The Jewish people, scattered all over the world today, are still zealously proud of heritage and ancestry.

I was to see a great deal of evidence of this, especially at the *Hadassah – Hebrew University Medical Centre* in Jerusalem, in the synagogue there.

The synagogue has become famous for the windows created by Marc Chagall which depict the origin of the twelve tribes of Israel. It was dedicated in 1961. The floors and interior walls are made of Jerusalem stone. It is illuminated by a hanging lantern and by sunlight which streams through the magnificent *Chagall Windows*.

Marc Chagall spoke of the joy he felt in bringing his gift to the Jewish people, who have always dreamt of biblical love, of friendship and peace among all people.

The windows are symbolic of the twelve sons of Jacob. Jacob's name was changed to Israel by God himself. Jacob means *supplanter*. Jacob supplanted the birthright of his brother Esau, from whom King Herod was descended. Israel means *soldier of God*, or *one who strives for God*. From the twelve sons of Jacob came the twelve tribes of Israel. Chagall's windows contain figures of animals, fish, flowers and numerous Jewish symbols. To understand the significance of the windows they must be viewed against Chagall's deep sense of identification with the whole of Jewish history, its tragedies and victories.

Each window has its own peculiar beauty but the dominant window is the window of Judah. This was inspired by Jacob's blessing on Judah.

'You, O Judah, your brothers shall praise;

Your hands shall be on the nape of your foes . . .

Judah is a lion's whelp . . .

The sceptre shall not depart from Judah' (Genesis 49.8–10).

The last line of that prophecy would have filled King Herod with fear when the wise men arrived in Jerusalem, seeking the child who had been born King of the Jews.

Herod would have surely consulted the Bethlehem census. From that, he would have learned that the wife of the direct living descendant of King David had borne a son in Bethlehem at the very time of the rising of the star, which the wise men had followed.

In his attempt to thwart that prophecy, Herod ordered the execution of the infant boys in Bethlehem, because the prophecies declared that the King who would restore the sceptre of Judah, would be born in Bethlehem.

Bethlehem is never mentioned again in the Gospels after the infancy narratives and there is no record of Jesus ever going back to the place of his birth in later years.

My first view of Bethlehem was from a kibbutz where the party with whom I was travelling stopped for lunch before going on to see the place where Mary gave birth to Jesus.

We looked across a wide valley to see the buildings of Bethlehem above terraces of olive groves, hugging the ridge on the other side. Towers of Christian churches and Moslem mosques dominated the skyline. Then we were driven on, six miles from Jerusalem, past the fields where the shepherds watched their flocks by night, up a steep hill to *The Church of the Nativity* which is described as the oldest church in the world.

After the destruction of Jerusalem in A.D. 70 Christians returned and identified many of the sites associated with Jesus Christ. In A.D. 135, the Emperor Hadrian attempted to obliterate these sites. He built a wall around the hill of Calvary, filled it in and on it built a temple to Venus. On the site, identified as the birth place of Jesus, he built a temple to Adonis. However, what Hadrian intended to bury forever he actually preserved, and located for future generations.

When Constantine made Christianity the religion of the Empire early in the fourth century, Hadrian's buildings were demolished and the sacred sites were unearthed.

The place where Mary gave birth to Jesus was found intact and Constantine surrounded it with a great church. This church was badly damaged in a revolt of Samaritans in 519, but it was rebuilt by the Emperor Justinian. It was the only church in the Holy Land which escaped destruction by the Persians in 614, when they embarked on a campaign to destroy all Christian buildings.

The Church of the Nativity was spared because the Persians found in it a mosaic representing the three wise men, in Persian dress.

There is only one entrance to *The Church of the Nativity* now. Two large doors were walled up, and the third was reduced to a small narrow opening, known as *The Eye of the Needle*. This was done to prevent men riding into the building on horseback, bent on destruction.

To enter the building it is necessary to bow low, as did the shepherds and wise men when they beheld the Christ child.

The grotto of Christ's birth dispels all the Christmas card conceptions one may have had of the Nativity. There was no quaint stable with clean convenient straw, but simply the hard earth shelter of a rugged cave in which a few animals could take refuge.

Before I left Australia I had promised two friends who were ill, that I should say special prayers for them in the Holy Land. People were lighting candles and placing them near the grotto. I acquired two candles and made them the outward visible sign of the prayers I offered for my friends. I left them glowing in the shadow of that place which had been illuminated by the Star of Bethlehem.

A silver star with the Latin inscription *Hic de Maria Virgine Jesus Christus natus est* (Here Jesus Christ was born of the Virgin Mary), marks the place where Mary gave her baby to the world. To the right of this place was the site of the manger, in which the baby was laid in swaddling clothes.

In the first chapter of his Gospel, St John states that the Son of God is the eternal Word by whom all things were made (John 1.3) and that the Word became flesh and dwelt among us (John 1.14).

St Paul wrote, 'in Christ was all the fulness of God embodied' (Colossians 2.9).

The title, *Mother of God*, in Greek, *Theotokos*, was given to Mary at *The Ecumenical Council of Ephesus* in 431. The title was given not so much as to honour Mary, but to emphasise the deity of Jesus Christ. Those who refuse to honour Mary as the Mother of God, cannot truly believe in the Incarnation.

When we have learned to accept God as our Father, we become his children, his sons and daughters by adoption, and such we become through the Sacrament of Baptism. Jesus Christ however, is the only begotten Son of God. In this sense, begotten means existing because of. Because the Father exists, the Son exists and has always existed.

God revealed himself through his creation, which he brought into being by the eternal Word and, in the fulness of time the Word became flesh. The fact of the Word becoming flesh is called the Incarnation.

Thus God, having revealed himself by what his Word had brought into being, revealed himself completely through the Word made flesh in Jesus Christ.

In *The Apostles' Creed*, in professing belief in the manner in which the Word became flesh, we say, 'He was conceived by the Holy Spirit, born of the Virgin Mary.'

Man has called the Creator *the Father* because in human terms, the father becomes the first cause of a new life by implanting the seed of life in the womb of a woman.

In the case of the Word of God becoming man, it was God himself who planted the seed of human life in the womb of the Blessed Virgin Mary of Nazareth.

'The Incarnation was not only the work of the Father, of his Power and his Spirit, but it was also the work of the will and faith of the Virgin. Just as God became incarnate voluntarily, so he wishes that his Mother should bear him freely and with her full consent.' (On the Annunciation – Patologia Orientalis, Vol. XIX. Nicholas Cabasilas.)

So, in *The Nicene Creed* we profess our belief that 'for us men and for our salvation he came down from Heaven and was incarnate by the Holy Ghost, of the Virgin Mary and was made man.'

Can anyone question why these words drive some people to their knees?

The wonder, the stupendous wonder of their meaning, seems to demand recognition in an act of human humility, because God has shown his great love for man by abandoning his heavenly glory, to share the life of man in complete humility in an act which holds time together.

This is the great fact which the Church calls us to celebrate on Christmas Day.

In some places the Incarnation is commemorated three times every day, at 6 a.m., midday and 6 p.m. by the saying of *The Angelus*. The church bell is rung eighteen times with three sequences of three strokes followed by nine strokes.

The great French artist Millet painted a picture, now very famous, which he called *The Angelus*.

Two peasants, a man and a woman, are depicted standing in a field. Their heads are bowed. The man is holding his hat. His hay fork has been stuck into the ground beside his barrow. The woman's hands are clasped in the attitude of prayer. The sun is setting over the hay stacks in the field. In the distance there is a church. It is to be understood that the man and the woman can hear the bell ringing the chimes of the Angelus and that they are commemorating the great act of God in the Incarnation of Jesus Christ.

As the Rosary is not an act of worship directed to the Blessed Virgin Mary, neither is the Angelus.

The Angelus is a commemoration of the Word of God becoming flesh.

On the first three strokes of the bell, the Annunciation is recalled with the words stating a fact of Holy Scripture —

'The Angel of the Lord brought the tidings to Mary and she conceived by the Holy Spirit.'

On the second set of three strokes of the bell, Mary's response is remembered.

'Behold the handmaid of the Lord, be it unto me, according to your Word.'

And as the third set of three strokes is chimed, the great fact of the Incarnation is stated.

'The Word became flesh and dwelt amongst us.'

Each section is followed by the saying of the *Hail Mary*.

Then as the bell is rung nine times, the collect for the Feast of Annunciation is said.

'Lord pour your grace into our hearts that as we have known the Incarnation of your Son, Jesus Christ, by the message of an angel, so by his cross and passion we may be brought to the glory of his resurrection.'

*   *   *

The fourth joyful mystery is the Presentation of Christ in the Temple.

> *Conscious of hidden Deity,*
> *The lowly Virgin brings*
> *Her new-born Babe, with two young doves*
> *Her tender offerings.*
>
> *The aged Simeon sees at last*
> *His Lord so long desired,*
> *And Anna welcomes Israel's hope*
> *With holy rapture fired.*

It was the custom for the parents of a first born son to offer a sacrifice forty days after his birth. The smallest acceptable offering in the temple was two pigeons. This was the offering of the very poor people. It was the offering of Mary and Joseph.

The wise men had not yet arrived with their gifts. At the time when Mary and Joseph took the forty days old child to Jerusalem, only Elizabeth and the humble shepherds had recognised him as the long promised Messiah.

When Joseph took Mary and her child from Bethlehem to Jerusalem, Mary might have expected a great welcome in the temple.

If the birth of the Messiah had been made known

by the angel to the shepherds who heard the angelic choir, would not God's messenger also have informed the High Priest of Israel that the ancient prophecy of Malachi was about to be fulfilled?

'The Lord whom you seek will suddenly come into his temple' (Malachi 3.1).

She was bringing the Lord to his temple. Would the High Priest lay aside his robes and do obeissance to the infant Jesus, and then announce that the Messianic reign had begun?

According to custom, the sacrifice was offered formally. The ceremonial of purification was performed, but there was no recognition by any of the priests.

Then an old man named Simeon stepped forward and took the baby in his arms. He was so old that it was believed that he could not die until he had seen the Messiah.

The identity of Mary's child was recognised, not by the great, not by the professional religionists, but by old Simeon who, like the humble shepherds, had the purity of heart to see the Lord.

Thirty years later Mary's Son was to say 'Blessed are the pure in heart for they shall see the Lord.' He spoke these words in what is called *The Sermon on the Mount*.

I have read them many times, but never have they moved me more than when I read them at the church which the Franciscans built on one of the hills overlooking the Sea of Galilee, to identify the place where Jesus first said them.

The group of which I was a member had crossed the

Sea of Galilee in a boat from Tiberius and had been taken to the hill known as the Mountain of the Beatitudes.

Our guide did not know who I was, or what I was, because I was wearing casual clothes. He approached me and asked if I might read something from *The Bible*. Of course I agreed and he showed me *St Matthew's Gospel*, chapter 5, verses 1–12.

'Perhaps you would like to practise,' he suggested.

I said it would not be necessary, and the crowd gathered around me.

I wanted to put the passage in its context so that those who heard it on the site where it was first uttered would understand better.

I told them that *The Sermon on the Mount* was our Lord's policy speech, and was to be found in chapters 5, 6 and 7 of St Matthew's Gospel. The words I was to read, I explained, were called *The Beatitudes* because they described the character to be striven for by those who desired to be citizens of the kingdom which Jesus had come to establish on earth. This kingdom, I said, was a kingdom of right relationships in which each cared for the others and ministered to their needs in love and truth.

It was a beautiful day. From where we were standing at the church, the sparkling waters of the Sea of Galilee could be seen through a terraced garden. And so I read the first twelve verses of the fifth chapter of *St Matthew's Gospel*.

Then I showed them what Jesus taught about receiving power to put the principles into practice.

'If we turn to the next chapter in *St Matthew's Gospel*,' I said, 'We can find the source of this power.' And I continued to read –

'When you pray, say, *Our Father, who art in Heaven.*' There was a moment of silence, then everyone joined in the prayer, and a group of people who hardly knew each other, found themselves united in a common bond, seeking to be blessed in their desire to be citizens of the kingdom.

Simeon opened his mouth and praised God in the words we know as the lovely evening canticle, *The Nunc Dimittis.*

'Lord now let your servant depart in peace according to your word

for I have seen, with my own eyes, your salvation

which will be for all people,

to be a light to lighten the Gentiles and the glory of

your people Israel.'

One of the great spiritual writers of the Anglican Communion, Father Andrew of the Society of the Divine Compassion, wrote a book *The Song of Simeon.* The following is a quotation from that book.

'Simeon standing with the divine child in his arms spoke for all who were ready to trust love in the hour of death. He held in his arms not only the light of God's revelation, but also the mystery of God's method. God's plan of salvation had its first revelation in the form of a human baby.

May God give us, to gladden our eyes in life and to lighten them in death, the vision of Simeon, standing with the divine child in his arms and the Blessed Mother kneeling at his side.'

Simeon spoke then as a faithful watchman who had been released from the duty he had completed.

Then he turned to Mary and told her that a sword of sorrow would pierce her own soul, and that her son would cause the rise and fall of many in Israel (Luke 2.35).

Simeon was joined by a strange old widow Anna, to whom the identity of the child had also been revealed.

She too invoked blessings on him and his mother.

Because old Simeon and Anna were pure in heart, God's purpose was fulfilled through them in their perception of the identity of the infant Jesus, and they were truly blessed.

Mary kept the memory of these events in her heart. Then she and Joseph took the infant Jesus back to Bethlehem.

It is not known how long they remained in Bethlehem. Joseph may have found a house there and a job, having decided to stay on.

Then came the wise men who had followed the star to present their gifts of gold, frankincense and myrrh. The gift of gold revealed that they knew the child had been born to be King of the Jews, the frankincense was to acknowledge his deity and the myrrh foretold his sacrifice.

When Herod the King determined to kill the child, Joseph was warned by God. He took Mary and Jesus to Egypt where they found refuge from Herod.

There have always been refugees from oppression. The Son of God began his life as a refugee.

The Holy Family remained in Egypt until Joseph

heard of Herod's death. He did not return to Bethlehem, but went back to Nazareth in Galilee, where Jesus grew through infancy into boyhood.

In the home at Nazareth, Joseph fulfilled his part in God's plan for man's salvation by giving the holy child such an example of human fatherhood as would enable him to grow in the knowledge of his Father in Heaven.

St Luke has given his testimony of the loving care of Mary and Joseph in the home at Nazareth.

And the child grew and waxed strong in spirit, filled with wisdom and the grace of God was upon him.

*   *   *

The fifth joyful mystery is the Finding of Jesus in the Temple.

> *Among the doctors see*
> *The Boy so full of grace;*
> *Say, wherefore taketh he*
> *The scholar's lowly place?*
> *That we may learn from pride to flee,*
> *And follow his humility.*

He was then at the age of twelve and he had been lost for three days.

The commemoration which had most influence on the lives of Jewish people was the Passover when they recalled their deliverance from Egypt hundreds of years before. It was not simply the memory of a past event, but the bringing of the past into the present.

The father would say to his family 'We were slaves in Egypt, we sacrificed an unblemished lamb in haste, and marked our houses with the blood. We fled from Egypt through the Red Sea on dry land after God's angel had passed over Egypt and the first born in every Egyptian family died.'

The father spoke as if he and the family had been present.

From the first celebration of the Passover onwards, every Jewish woman presented her first born son to God, when he was forty days old, in thanksgiving that the first born sons of the Israelites in Egypt had been delivered from death by the blood of the lamb on the door posts of their houses.

When a Jewish boy reached the age of twelve he was, if possible, taken to Jerusalem to be admitted into the adult life of his religion. A visit to the temple formed a part of this event.

So Jesus who had been presented to God in the temple as a forty days old baby was again taken to the temple at the age of twelve to be recognised as an adult member of his religion.

When I first saw Jerusalem I found that so many of the psalms which I had been saying for as long as I can remember suddenly came to life. Indeed as I journeyed through the whole of Israel, I realised how the psalmists had caught the vision of the glory of creation and reproduced that vision in sublime poetry.

As Jesus grew up in Nazareth, those glorious sunrises and sunsets casting ever changing colours and shadows on the surrounding countryside would have enabled him to sing – 'Praise the Lord, O my soul – O Lord my God, thou art become exceeding glorious, thou art clothed with majesty and honour – Thou deckest thyself with light as it were a garment and spreadest out the heavens like a curtain.'

I have never been so conscious of the curve of the horizon and the dome of the sky, anywhere in the world, as I was in the Holy Land. It is a hard land with bold contours but it is made beautiful by the light of the sun and the moon, and the rains that fall on it make it rich in providing food for man and beast. The psalmist caught the splendour of it all and sang, 'The glorious majesty of the Lord shall endure for ever.'

Jesus as a boy of twelve, going to Jerusalem, would have travelled from Nazareth along the hot and dusty route travelled by his mother and Joseph before his birth, to Aenon, parallel with the Jordan River and on to Jericho which is on a large oasis, described today as the oldest and deepest city in the world, 850 feet below sea level.

Travelling along this route one does not see the river. The streams which flow into it make the terrain along it too rugged for a road, so the road is some distance from the river.

Beside the tarred road today there is a dirt road, which runs along the wire fence which separates Israel from Jordan. Every evening an army truck sweeps the unsealed road and every morning, down the entire length of Israel, the road is examined for foot prints of Jordanians who might have entered Israel illegally.

In Jesus' day there was no barricade and no road, only the wide trade route.

Behind Jericho rises the Mountain of Qarantal, which is believed to be the wilderness where eighteen years later Jesus was to experience the temptation of

Satan, following his baptism by John and the sub-
sequent forty days fast. From the top of this mountain
he would have a magnificent view of the Jordan Valley
and the land of Moab. Looking over this vast view, he
would hear Satan say, 'I will give you the kingdoms of
the world if you will worship me.'

Leaving Jericho, Jesus would have made the ascent
through the foreboding hills in which the robbers he
was to tell about in his parable, *The Good Samaritan*,
lurked to prey upon lonely travellers. He would have
passed that which is still the only inn along the road, a
shabby rest house in the arid hills called now *The Inn
of the Good Samaritan*.

He would have passed through Bethany where
about twenty one years later he was to raise his friend
Lazarus from the dead.

Then he would have seen Jerusalem, on the hill of
Zion, surrounded by much loftier and grander hills. In
years to come he was to look down on the city from
one of these lofty hills and weep over it, knowing the
faithlessness of its people.

The psalmist saw the Hill of Zion, the dwelling
place of God, as a sign of the humility of God, and he
saw the higher hills as the symbols of arrogancy and
pride.

'The Hill of Zion is fair place, and the joy of all the
earth.' (Psalm 48.2)

'Why hop ye so, ye high hills – This (lowly Mount
Zion) is the Lord's hill in which he is pleased to dwell.'
(Psalm 68.16)

The hills around Jerusalem were also seen as the
symbols of the presence of God. 'The hills stand about

Jerusalem; even so standeth the Lord round his people.' (Pslam 25.2).

So, as Jesus made his way to Jerusalem on the threshold of his adult life, he would sing with the other pilgrims –

'I was glad when they said unto me, we shall go into the house of the Lord.' (Psalm 122.1).

When I was in Israel, I was taken to *The University of Bar Ilam* not far from Tel Aviv. Here we saw *The Museum of the Diaspora*, showing the scattering of Jews throughout the world, beginning with the countries around the Mediterranean Sea.

In this great Museum many facets of Jewish life are depicted by cycloramas.

I was impressed by one scene, with figures of men, women and children in the synagogues and in the homes, which emphasised the duty of instructing the young. The instruction of the young was to be regarded as the sacred duty and privilege of all adults.

With this in mind it is easy to understand why the learned teachers of the Law were so willing to spend their time, instructing the twelve year old Jesus and answering his questions. We can imagine too just how many questions he had to ask, about the Passover, and the many festivals which were celebrated in the temple, and the history of his people.

While I was in Jerusalem, the people were preparing for the Feast of Tabernacles, the most joyous of all festivals. Everywhere shelters were being constructed over which branches of palm and olive leaves were being laid for a covering.

The festival still celebrates the completion of the harvest and commemorates the dwelling in tents or booths during the wandering in the wilderness.

In the days of the temple, the lighting of the golden candlesticks in *The Women's Court* was a great feature of this festival. During this ceremony, Jesus was to proclaim himself as the light of the world.

The temple no longer exists. It was destroyed in A.D. 70 and since then Jerusalem has had many occupants. On the site of the temple today stands the huge mosque, called *The Dome of the Rock*.

The Dome of the Rock was originally built at the end of the seventh century when the Moslems occupied the city. It ranks as the third most important shrine of the Moslem world today, but it also stands as a witness of the common origin of Judaism and Mohammedanism.

The great dome made from a bronze alloy which makes it shine like gold in the Jerusalem sunshine, stands above *the rock*, believed to be the peak of Mount Moriah on which Abraham prepared to sacrifice his son Isaac. The Arabs, most of whom are Moslems, claim their descent from Abraham through Ishmael, the son of his slave woman, Hagar. When the temple of the Jews stood on this site, *the rock* served as the altar for the burnt offerings. There is a hole in *the rock* through which the blood of the sacrifices of the old covenant was drained.

After removing shoes and entering the huge building rich in mosaics, woodwork and gilded pillars, one is almost overwhelmed by the silence. The shrine stands on a plateau. Below on the west side, there is a large esplanade separated from the higher area on which *The*

Dome of the Rock stands, by a wall. This wall is the only remnant of the Jews' temple which was destroyed in A.D. 70.

The wall with the large pavement area to the west of it belongs to the Jews, but the higher area on the Eastern side where the Mosque stands is the property of the Moslems.

Devout Jews pray standing facing the wall, the men at one end and the women and children at the other. A boy cannot join the men until he has been acknowledged as an adult member of his faith, as Jesus was when he went to Jerusalem at the age of twelve.

I went to the wall on the Sabbath. The wall used to be called *The Wailing Wall*, but since the Jewish victory in 1967 and the capture of Jerusalem, the people no longer bewail the loss of the city. But they come to the remnant of the temple, to touch the wall and to pray. Many write out their prayers and wedge them into the crevices where one stone rests on another.

Many pray aloud alone. Some continually bump their heads on the wall as they pray. People move about, oblivious of each other. Some form groups and pray together. A group must consist of ten adult men. Some wear black suits with long coats and large black hats, others wear long garments and shawls with strings. All men have their heads covered, either with skull caps or hats of fur or felt.

It was easy to imagine the court of the old temple with people moving about, standing praying aloud, and think of a twelve year old boy surrounded by a group of heavily bearded men wearing shawls, head coverings and phylacteries, listening to them and asking them questions.

So it becomes clear why the finding of the boy Jesus
in the temple at the age of twelve after he had been lost
for three days was a joyful mystery. It was joyful
because the missing boy was found. This was the joy of
relief from anxiety. It was joyful because of the
impression that Jesus made on the wise men of his own
race. They were amazed at his understanding and
answers. This was the joy of a mother's pride in her
son.

It was joyful because Jesus assured his mother that
he was about his Father's business. This is the joy of
satisfaction for the fulfilment of her vocation as his
mother and for Joseph's vocation as his guardian.

Twenty one years later, during Passover, Mary's
heart was to be saddened again by the loss of her son,
but on the third day we may think of him coming to her
with the same words he spoke in the temple when he
was twelve –

'How is it that you sought me, didn't you know
that I must be about my Father's business?'

Mary and Joseph brought the twelve year old Jesus
to the temple for the Passover just as Christian parents
might bring their children of that age to confirm the
faith which their godparents had professed for them,
and to promise to spend their lives about the business
of their Heavenly Father, with his blessing imparted
through the laying on of hands by a bishop, one of the
leaders of today's church.

The visit to the Passover Festival in Jerusalem with
the twelve year old boy was a part of his growing up. It
was to mark the beginning of his adult life.

Mary and Joseph took Jesus back to Nazareth
where St Luke tells us in his Gospel that he increased in

wisdom and in stature and in favour with God and man (Luke 2.52).

Jesus was truly human. He had no advantage over any one of us.

He asked questions of the learned men in the temple. He did not know everything right from the beginning. He had to learn like any other boy. He increased in wisdom.

He grew physically, he increased in stature.

He increased in favour with his Heavenly Father. Eighteen years later at his baptism by Elizabeth's son John, his Father would declare that he was well pleased with him.

And he increased in favour with man. It would be said of him that the common people heard him gladly.

And this is how we should all endeavour to grow, as St Paul wrote in *The Epistle to the Ephesians*,

'until we come to the unity of the faith and of the knowledge of the Son of God to a perfect being, to the measure of the stature of the fulness of Christ.' (Ephesians 4.13).

CHAPTER THREE

Bearing the Pain

(The Sorrowful Mysteries)

The first of the sorrowful mysteries is the Agony in the Garden of Gethsemane.

> *Go to dark Gethsemane,*
> *Ye that feel the Tempter's power*
> *Your Redeemer's conflict see,*
> *Watch with him one bitter hour:*
> *Turn not from his griefs away,*
> *Learn of Jesus Christ to pray.*

The Garden of Gethsemane is one of the few sites in the Jerusalem area which is seen today much as it was in the time of our Lord. Indeed, it is said that some of the gnarled olive trees growing there now were there two thousand years ago.

The garden is cared for by the Franciscan friars who try to maintain it as it was. The Franciscans also have a church nearby in which there are murals depicting the agony and the betrayal of Jesus by Judas.

In the Garden of Gethsemane I felt that the time was too fleeting as I tried to visualise the events there, and the agony of Jesus.

The agony in the garden occurred after the Last Supper. I had been to the chapel which identifies the place of the upper room where Jesus took the bread and wine, designating the elements to be his body and blood. The chapel is above the tomb of David, near *The Zion Gate* into the old city.

I was in the chapel at mid-day and *The Angelus* was rung to commemorate the Incarnation – the Word becoming flesh to dwell amongst us. There was I, standing at the place where the Word of God in human flesh, by his word, gave bread to be his flesh and wine to be his blood, that he might continually dwell in us and we in him.

After the supper, during which Judas had gone out into the night, Jesus and the eleven disciples sang a hymn and then went to the Mount of Olives.

This walk in the light of the Passover full moon took them along the south wall and over the Kedron Valley and past the tomb of Absolom.

The Garden of Gethsemane lies at the foot of the Mount of Olives which looks stark and eerily beautiful in the silent moonlight.

There Jesus prayed and experienced great agony.

The agony in the garden was greater than the agony of the crucifixion because for the first time in his life he prayed a prayer expressing his own will which was contrary to the will of his Father.

'O my Father, if it be possible let this cup pass from me.'

But, according to the will of his Father, it was not possible, because he had sent his Son into the world to be truly human, to endure the consequences of the will of man and to be obedient in his humanity, even to death on the cross.

When we pray, we should always remember the agony of Christ in the Garden of Gethsemane.

The purpose of prayer is not for what I want or what you want in a particular situation, but that God's will may be done.

Mary submitted herself to the will of God at the Annunciation when she said, 'Behold the handmaid of the Lord. Let it be to me, according to your word.'

When our Lord prayed in the garden, his disciples fell asleep and, in the agony of his humanity, he qualified his prayer, 'Not my will, but your will be done.'

The agony our Lord experienced in the garden was not the anticipation of physical pain, but the consequences of human sin and the betrayal and the faithlessness of the disciples who had quarrelled over who should be chief among them.

The late Scottish theologian William Barclay said that there was something of infinite beauty and infinite value in St Mark's account of the agony in Gethsemane. Barclay emphasised that, according to Mark Jesus addressed his Father as *Abba*, which was how a very young child would address his father in the intimate family circle.

In the agony, Jesus spoke to his Father as an infant would speak to a father whom he loved and trusted.

St Luke tells us that an angel came to strengthen him.

An angel is a messenger from God and there is a

suggestion, although with not a great deal of foundation, that the messenger from God in the garden was Mary. She could have found out what Judas intended to do. She would have been very close to all that was happening. When they went to the garden, would it not have been a natural reaction for an anxious mother, who had probably been downstairs with the other women during the Last Supper, to follow?

St Mark tells us that a lad followed Jesus and the apostles, and was nearly caught (Mark 14.51). This lad was possibly Mark himself.

In the story of Mary being the messenger from God in the garden, she tells Jesus that Mark brought her to the garden. She reminds her son that he was named Jesus because he would save the people from their sins.

'Whatever you do my son,' she says, 'will be for the salvation of your people.'

Jesus replies, 'It is the Passover feast, and I am the priest, but as John the Baptist said, I am also the Lamb.'

'Yes,' says Mary, 'The Lamb of God who takes away the sins of the world.'

In the story, Jesus, aware of the danger, sends his mother away and resumes his prayer, using the words recorded by St John in the seventeenth chapter –

> 'Father, the hour has come, glorify your son, that your son may glorify you. I have finished the work which you gave me to do.'

Then Judas arrives with the temple guard to betray his Lord.

The account of the arrest, written by all four evangelists is very vivid.

'Whom do you seek,' asks Jesus.

The temple guards reply, 'Jesus of Nazareth.'

'I am he,' says Jesus, and they all fall to the ground because he has uttered the name of God, *Jehovah* which in Hebrew means *I am that I am.*

A skirmish breaks out. With a sword Peter cuts off the ear of the High Priest's servant. Jesus heals him and tells Peter to put away the sword. Judas betrays Jesus with a kiss and the disciples run off in panic as Jesus is arrested.

*   *   *

The second sorrowful mystery is the Scourging of our Lord.

> *See him at the judgement-hall,*
> *Beaten, bound, reviled, arraigned;*
> *See him meekly bearing all!*
> *Love to man his soul sustained.*
> *Shun not suffering, shame, or loss;*
> *Learn of Christ to bear the Cross.*

Judas had betrayed him, Peter had denied him and the others had forsaken him and fled from him in the garden. He had faced trials before the High Priest Caiaphas and his father-in-law, the emeritus High Priest Annas, with *The Sanhedrin* (the Council of Seventy); before Pontius Pilate; before Herod Antipas, who mocked him and sent him back to Pilate.

Pilate had been unable to find Jesus guilty of any of the accusations against him but, hoping to pacify the High Priest who would threaten to bring the wrath of Caesar on him if he favoured Jesus, he ordered him to be scourged.

The site where the merciless scourging with the cruel Roman whip took place, is identified in Jerusalem today by *The Chapel of the Flagellation*.

The chapel contains mural paintings of scenes depicting the trial and the scourging of Jesus. The whip is depicted with all its horror, its leather thongs studded with pieces of metal to tear the flesh of the victim.

Although a number of buildings have occupied the site since Jesus was scourged, the pillar to which the victim was bound is represented.

It is not likely that Mary would have witnessed the scourging, but she would have seen the result of it when she saw her son stripped of his clothing for the crucifixion. The pain she bore then was great indeed.

The scourging of Jesus fulfilled the prophecy of Isaiah, 'The punishment that brought us peace was upon him. By his stripes we are healed' (Isaiah 53.5, 6).

*   *   *

The third sorrowful mystery is Jesus being crowned with thorns.

> *O sacred head, sore wounded,*
> *Defiled and put to scorn;*
> *O kingly head, surrounded*

With mocking crown of thorn:
What sorrow mars thy grandeur?
Can death thy bloom de flower?
O countenance whose splendour
The hosts of heaven adore.

After the soldiers had scourged Jesus, they mocked him. They threw a purple cloak over his bleeding shoulders; they plaited a crown of thorns and forced it on his head, scratching and tearing his flesh.

Opposite *The Chapel of the Flagellation* is *The Pavement*, known by its Greek name, *Lithostrotos*. It is believed that the paving stones are those on which Jesus stood before Pontius Pilate as he sat in the judgement hall and handed him over to be crucified.

Nearby is an archway called *The Arch of Ecce Homo. Ecce Homo* is Latin for *Behold the Man.* The arch identifies the site where Jesus was brought from the place of the scourging wearing the crown of thorns and the purple robe, and Pilate said, 'Behold the man!'

When Pontius Pilate presented him to the jeering crowd, Mary would have seen him. How Simeon's sword would have pierced her soul then.

'Behold the man!' cried Pilate.

Then Pilate brought forward Barabbas the robber and murderer, and asked the people to choose which prisoner they wanted to be released as a Passover favour. The crowds, by a strong majority vote, demanded the release of Barabbas and the death of Jesus.

Pontius Pilate called for a basin, washed his hands and delcared himself to be innocent of the blood of that just man.

The crowd shouted, 'His blood be on us and on our children!' and Pilate handed him over to the army, to crucify him.

According to the historian Josephus, the closing years of Pontius Pilate's governorship of Judea were marked by an increasing number of acts of cruelty to the Jews, which even Rome could not tolerate. He was removed from his office and subsequently took his own life.

Pilate was a man who was corrupted by power.

It seems that he had much in common with Hitler, who was directly responsible for the murder of six million Jews, between 1933 and 1945.

In Jerusalem there is a national memorial to the Jews who perished during the Nazi regime in Europe. It is *Yad Vashem*, a very imposing building in the centre of which is a shrine and an archive chamber where the records of those who perished are being collected and preserved on file.

We approached the building through an avenue of trees. This is called *The Avenue of the Righteous Gentiles*. It is a tribute to those who were not Jews, who helped to save Jewish lives during that terrible period which is now known as *The Holocaust*.

Inside the building there is an eerie silence, vastly different from the silence in *The Dome of the Rock*. Perhaps this silence is better described as a hush which, if broken by the slightest sound, might give way to six million agonising screams of death.

Some of Israel's leading artists have made their contributions to the memorial in sculptures and paintings, all of which symbolise the agony and tyranny of

The Holocaust. The walls of several halls are lined with photographs. Most of them were taken by the Nazis themselves. These depict the cruelest and most barbarous treatment of men, women and children ever known.

The pictures are gruesome records of the degrading humiliation of human beings before they died in the most vile and disgusting manner.

Six million people were exterminated for no other reason than that they were Jews.

Those who were most degraded were not the victims of the diabolical mass extermination, but the perpetrators of it. The great tragedy is that these were ordinary members of the community, well educated men who in peace time had lived normal lives as husbands and fathers. However, convinced by the Nazi philosophy that every Jew was a powerful enemy of the German people, they went about their terrible work with fanatical zeal and cruel precision.

Pontius Pilate was a man like any of them and, like them his power made him a cruel tyrant.

Such places as *Yad Vashem* in Jerusalem, should challenge all people to strive to live in peace and unity, so that such happenings as they commemorate will never occur again. However, there is a danger that the hatred roused by the perpetuation of the memories of those evil days will be passed on down the ages.

Let us remember the past, but let us remember such events in the light of the teaching of Jesus.

> 'Love your enemies, do good to those who persecute you and do all manner of evil against you, that you may be children of my Father.'

And let us hear the words of his mother.

'Whatever he says to you, do it.'

*   *   *

The fourth sorrowful mystery is Jesus bearing the cross.

> *Heavy that Cross to him*
> *Weary the weight:*
> *One who will help him stands*
> *At the gate.*
> *Multitudes hurrying*
> *Pass on the road:*
> *Simon is sharing with*
> *Him the load.*

The cross was laid upon the bleeding shoulder of Jesus and he began to carry it along *The Way of Sorrows* to the Hill of Calvary.

To walk along that way today in Jerusalem, *The Via Dolorosa, The Sorrowful Way*, is not an easy progress. Bustling, pushing crowds throng the narrow streets, so steeply inclined that steps are necessary in certain places. People of all ages and types, classes and creeds vie with each other to maintain their chosen direction. Bearded priests in black from head to foot, mingle with white robed Arabs. Sombrely clad Jews with long ringlets of hair falling across their faces under large black hats, are brushed aside by bare footed urchins selling 40 postcards for a shekel. Tourists from many lands identify themselves by their accents and the languages they speak.

Arab boys weave their way through the crowds with easy skill, balancing on their heads trays filled with bread rolls, pies or fish, while others push box carts with bicycle wheels up the hill. These carts are laden with enormous dates and figs, pomegranates, huge bunches of grapes, melons or pastry or fish. For the downhill journey the boys seem to be dragged along by the carts. They slow them down by jumping on a rubber bicycle tyre, tied by a rope to the cart, trailing along the ground behind it. They call out 'hello, hello,' to make the crowds divide to let them through.

Shopkeepers sit or stand in the doorways of their stores, trying to lure the tourists within, to purchase their silks, brassware and wood carvings.

Although the buildings along that way have changed, Jesus would have carried his cross through the narrow streets thronged by the same kind of pushing, indifferent people, to whom his passing by meant nothing at all.

Has any mother suffered more than Mary suffered along *The Way of Sorrows?* The traditional picture is of her being supported by John and Mary Magdalene, coming face to face with her son, as she followed him to Calvary.

How hard was it for her then, to see any meaning in the message of the angel, that he would be great and would be called the Son of the Highest, and of his kingdom there would be no end.

Jesus carried the cross through the crowded thoroughfare, weakened by the loss of blood and lack of food. He was truly human and he collapsed under the weight of the cross. The soldiers compelled a bystander, Simon of Cyrene, to carry the cross for Jesus.

Along *The Way of Sorrows* today. Some of the fourteen Stations of the Cross can be seen. These are stone carvings of the events they commemorate, set in the walls of buildings.

The first of the stations is in the *Lithostrotos*, Pilate's judgement hall, where Jesus was condemned to be crucified. The last five stations are in *The Church of the Holy Sepulchre.*

The Stations of the Cross are related to the sorrowful mysteries. The carrying of the cross by Simon of Cyrene, is marked by the fifth station. The first four are the condemnation of Jesus, the receiving of the cross, the first fall and Jesus meeting his mother. The other nine are the wiping of Jesus' face by Veronica, the second fall, Jesus meeting the women of Jerusalem, the third fall, the stripping of Jesus' clothes, the nailing to the cross, the death of Jesus, the removal of the dead body of Jesus from the cross and finally the burial of the body in Joseph of Arimathaea's tomb.

It seems that Simon of Cyrene became a follower of Jesus Christ.

Mark wrote his Gospel mainly for Christian people in Rome. He identified Simon of Cyrene as the father of Alexander and Rufus. This seems to indicate that when Mark wrote his Gospel, Alexander and Rufus were prominent members of the church in Rome. When St Paul wrote to the Christians in Rome, he mentioned a person named Rufus, who was possibly a son of Simon. Paul also had a companion in Ephesus named Alexander. Moreover two of the leaders of the church in Antioch, when Paul and Barnabas left on their first missionary journey, were Simon and Lucius of Cyrene.

For Simon of Cyrene, to carry the cross of a

condemned criminal would have at first been a distasteful task, but it was completed as an honoured privilege.

Closely associated with Simon of Cyrene carrying the cross, is the tradition that a woman named Veronica wiped the face of Jesus. Simon carried the cross and Veronica also did what she could to ease his suffering.

A great spiritual truth is proclaimed by this tradition commemorated by the sixth Station of the Cross.

As Jesus staggered along *The Via Dolorosa*, some women of Jerusalem wept for him. According to the tradition, one of them, seeing the blood and sweat streaming down his face, was moved to do something practical about her tears. In an act of compassion, she wiped his face to give what little comfort she could, and the imprint of his face remained on the cloth she used.

Veronica ministered to Jesus and found his face in the object with which she served him.

Just as it was through the obedience of the Blessed Virgin Mary that God in human flesh was manifested to the world, so in every act, where the law of loving compassion is obeyed, the face of Christ is revealed.

I had an experience of this in one of the most deprived places in South Africa, in the township of Alexandra near Johannesburg.

Alexandra is the scene of much of the tragic activity in Alan Paton's book *Cry the Beloved Country*. It is also part of the background in Bishop Trevor Huddleston's book *Naught for Your Comfort* which was first published in 1956. In it the bishop wrote:

'The boys of Alexandra are rotting away in over-crowded yards, in the dusty streets, at the corners and in the alleys because they cannot get work even if they want to.'

I went to Alexandra in 1983, twenty seven years after those lines were written. It was still the same.

I was driven there by a courageous Christian lady, who was going there regularly to give friendship and food to those whom social workers told her were the most needy in an area where there was dire poverty, sickness and crime.

White people visiting an area designated for black dwellings were required to get a permit to do so, but this lady refused to get a permit to visit fellow human beings. Once when challenged by the police who said she needed a permit for her own protection, she said, 'I am protected by the Lord Jesus Christ.' With her and without a permit, I visited a number of homes. 'The car is insured against stones,' she told me, 'but I am not.'

Immediately across the boundary of Alexandra we left the tarred road and entered the dusty unmade streets. Not a blade of grass could be seen. No pavements, no gutters, no kerbing. Dirty water ran down the slope of the road. I was warned to avoid treading in the mud as there was no sanitation. The fences where they existed were the broken doors of old cars or rusty corrugated iron.

There were a few shops. These were unpainted houses with a wider opening and a few posters and signs advertising familiar products in front.

The undertaker's parlour was obvious by the coffins in front, on the earthen space between the entrance and the road. It was as dirty as the other buildings.

'Brighter Funerals,' said the sign in front, 'Somebody has to bury you – why not let us do it?'

We pulled up in front of a house. A dozen or more black people stood and stared as we proceeded with parcels of food along the dusty path to the hovel. We knocked on the door and a black woman shuffled out to admit us. She did not raise her eyes to me. Her children had no such inhibitions and were eager to see what we had brought.

The black woman said she was feeling ill and sat down in a rickety, broken chair, staring at the bare floor. Her black woolly head was uncovered.

'The pastor from Australia will say a prayer for you,' said my companion.

Then the black woman raised her sad eyes to me. Because it was the custom of her people for women to cover their heads for prayer, she reached across and picked up an old matted woollen scarf. She drew it over her head and clasped her hands. Jesus Christ said, 'Where two or three are gathered together in my name, I am in the midst.' As the three of us bowed in prayer, I knew he was there, because I saw his face in the black face beneath the matted woollen scarf.

Was there much difference between Veronica's cloth and that woollen scarf?

I may have seen his face in the face beneath the scarf, but he was really present through the one who was serving him.

The great spiritual truth which the sixth station proclaims is that we shall see the face of Christ in the faces of those to whom we minister in loving service.

Simon of Cyrene carrying the cross upon which

was to hang the Saviour of the world, should inspire all who would follow Christ, to be ready to carry his cross in the name of suffering humanity.

Simon carried the cross through the gate of Jerusalem to the hill of Calvary.

Those who would take up his cross today must be prepared to carry it beyond the walls of ease and security, if necessary into the degradation of human misery.

Simon did not seek to find Jesus in the carrying of his cross. The cross was forced upon him, but we are continually being challenged to look for him in the lives of those who are bearing the crosses of racial hatred, of poverty, of sickness, of frustration and tyranny, stumbling and falling under the weight of the crosses they bear. When we have so found him, let us take up their crosses and carry them for Christ.

*   *   *

The last of the sorrowful mysteries is the Crucifixion.

> *How fast His Hands and Feet are nail'd;*
> *His Throat with parching thirst is dried*
> *His failing Eyes are dimm'd with Blood;*
> *Jesus, our Lord, is crucified.*
> *Seven times He spake, seven Words of love;*
> *And all three hours His silence cried*
> *For mercy on the souls of men;*
> *Jesus, our Lord, is crucified.*

There can be no more intimate way of understanding the Crucifixion than through the seven utterances of Jesus from the cross.

The first of these was 'Father forgive them they know not what they do.'

In this prayer our Lord expressed the intention of his sacrifice. He died that we might be forgiven.

This prayer reaches out, down the ages, beyond those in the immediate circle of the cross, beyond Judas who betrayed him, the disciples who fled, Peter who denied him, Caiaphas the High Priest who demanded his death, Pontius Pilate who condemned him, Herod who mocked him, the soldiers who ridiculed him, scourged him and crowned him with thorns, and the crowds who scorned him and rejected him. The prayer of Jesus reaches down the ages to us today and every day.

When our Lord came to John the Baptist at the River Jordan, John pointed to him and said, 'Behold the Lamb of God who takes away the sins of the world.'

On the hill called Calvary, Jesus fulfilled that prophecy.

He is the Lamb of God who reveals in his sacrifice, the infinite love of God for each one of us, no matter how unlovely or unlovable we may be.

God is love, and love for our sakes, in his own body, bore our sins on the cross.

I have sat with a mother in a court room when she heard the judge sentence her son to prison. I have seen her love for him as she bore the shame and the disgrace of his crime and in her then, I caught the glimpse of the love of God revealed in Jesus when, bearing our sins he prayed, 'Father forgive them, they know not what they do.'

The second utterance of Jesus from the cross was

his promise to the penitent thief, 'Today you shall be with me in Paradise.'

The two thieves who were crucified with Jesus were probably arrested with Barabbas in a riot during the Passover.

Barabbas obviously was a popular figure who was prepared to murder and plunder in his efforts to over-throw the Romans and establish an independent Jewish kingdom.

Pontius Pilate had placed on the cross of Jesus the title, *Jesus of Nazareth, King of the Jews*. This was done as a slight to Caiaphas the High Priest, who objected to it.

However that title also caused the crowd to mock Jesus, crying out, 'If you are the King of the Jews, save yourself – come down and we shall believe.'

The two thieves who were crucified with him also mocked him, but suddenly one of them changed. He had caught a glimpse of another kingdom.

It was probably his desire for a kingdom of this world, with Barabbas on the throne, that had brought this thief to the cross. He saw the title, 'King' written over the cross of the man beside him. *Jesus of Nazareth, King of the Jews*, which was written in Greek, Latin and Hebrew.

It is possible that the thief was a zealot, who had spent his life trying to overthrow the Roman oppressor and establish the Kingdom of the Jews.

The zealots were men of great courage and deter-mination. One of the twelve apostles, the other Simon, was a zealot.

In the barren wilderness of Judea, the foreboding

boulder strewn mountains seem to roll into each other like gigantic waves in a brown ocean of dry rocks.

None of the mountains is more stark nor more ominous than Masada, whose flat top rises 1300 feet above the Dead Sea.

On this hard rock plateau Herod the Great had built a fortress which was famous as an architectural and constructional wonder. Cisterns were hollowed out in caves, and water from occasional rains, so heavy as to cause rock avalanches, was channelled into them. An abundance of food was stored to feed the many guests who came to enjoy the luxury of the enormous complex.

A few years before the destruction of Jerusalem by the Romans in A.D. 70, a band of zealots led by Eleazar Ben Yair, captured Masada from the Roman Garrison and used it as a base for guerilla warfare until A.D. 73.

Today thousands of tourists visit Masada. Many use its winding snake pathway in an arduous climb, while the not so energetic can ascend to its height in a cable car, as I did.

From the top can be seen the outlines of the eight Roman siege camps from which the Roman General Silva, waged his campaign to recapture what seemed to be an impregnable fortress, with provisions to feed its occupants, for years.

Silva built an enormous earthen ramp up the side of the mountain, by means of which he assailed the walls. Eleazar Ben Yair, realising that this was the beginning of the end, urged his zealots to die by their own hands rather than become Roman prisoners.

When the Romans entered the fortress, all of its occupants, except two women and five children, were dead. The women told the Romans of the courage of the zealots whose deaths made the Roman victory a very hollow one.

The penitent thief displayed the same type of courage as he died.

It seems that this man knew Jesus. He rebuked the other thief.

'Don't you fear God,' he cried. 'We deserve our punishment, but this man has done no wrong.'

These words imply that he knew that Jesus had lived as a king should live, and now he could see that he was dying as a king should die. Then he addressed the King. 'Jesus,' he said.

In the New Testament narrative the penitent thief is the only person who addressed our Lord simply as *Jesus*.

Mary called him, *Son*. Those in need called him *Jesus, Master or Jesus, Son of David*. His disciples called him *Master, Teacher, Rabbi* or *Lord*. But the penitent thief called him *Jesus*.

The translators of *The Authorised Version* from the Greek, *The King James Bible*, took it upon themselves to change the thief's mode of address from *Jesus* to *Lord*. They felt it savoured of familiarity for the thief to call the dying king *Jesus*. But in the original Greek it stands as evidence that the thief understood the meaning of his name. 'He shall be called *Jesus*, because he will save his people from their sins' (Matthew 1.21).

And the thief said, 'Jesus, remember me when you come into your Kingdom.' And back came the certainty of it – the promise of Jesus. 'Today you will be with me in Paradise.'

It has been said that after our Lord's reassuring words to him, the penitent thief represented the whole of the Christian Church, for he alone at that time, had any conception of Christ's Kingdom – and the forgiveness of sins from the cross of Christ. Not even St John, or Mary herself, had any such vision of *The Kingdom*, at that moment. Only the dying thief beside him had caught a vision of a kingdom, not of this world, and he alone had been admitted by the King himself, baptised in his own blood.

The disciples would be admitted in a few days by the risen Lord who would breathe upon them and say, 'Peace be with you. As my Father has sent me even so I send you – Receive the Holy Ghost. Whose sins you forgive they are forgiven and whose sins ye retain they are retained.' But in his dying hour, only the penitent thief had been admitted, because only he had shown the necessary faith.

The third utterance of our Lord from the cross involved his mother directly in the fifth sorrowful mystery, as she stood by the cross with John the beloved disciple.

'Woman behold your son, Son behold your mother.'

In the context of the original Greek in which these words were written, our Lord's address to his mother as *Woman*, was an address of love, tenderness and respect.

We have already seen that his address to his Father in the Garden of Gethsemane as *Abba*, was one of deep affection. His address to his mother from the cross contained the same kind of affection.

The presence of Mary with John, at the cross makes

us realise indeed who it was who hung upon the cross. He was the *Word of God*; the creative force of God, by whom all things were made, who had existed from all eternity and was made flesh in the womb of Mary.

John wrote in the first chapter of his Gospel, 'The Word was made flesh and dwelt among us.'

The Word was made flesh because the Blessed Virgin Mary co-operated with God – and John, the writer of *The Fourth Gospel* gave us the account of it. The two stood together, she whom God used to enable his Word to become flesh, and he who translated the life of God in the flesh into his living word. 'In the beginning was the Word' wrote John, 'and the Word was made flesh and dwelt amongst us.'

No words of deeper meaning have ever been written. The opening phrase *in the beginning* carries our minds not merely back to the beginning of time, but beyond time and space to the initiation of all things. The words might be translated *at the back of everything*. The word *was* is also timeless, implying a mode of existence without beginning and without end.

The great acts of Jesus' life recorded by John, are but an expression in time of his eternal nature. He always brought to those who saw him a new birth. The penitent thief mocked him with the others at first, then, suddenly he saw him and, because he saw him, his sufferings became a common bond with the Word of God made flesh, and he received the assurance of life.

'The Word was made flesh and dwelt among us,' wrote John – and he continued, 'and we beheld his glory – the glory as of the only begotten of the Father, full of grace and truth.'

When was the glory of the Son of God more vivid than in his dying hours?

Unselfish to the last, his first thought was for his enemies – 'Father forgive them.' His next thought for his companion in death, 'Today you shall be with me in Paradise;' then his consideration for his own earthly mother. Seeing John and his mother together at the cross, Jesus said, 'Woman behold your son, son behold your mother.' His unselfish glory shone out through the pain.

Yet Mary's son knew how she felt and, from the cross his love reached down to her.

He knew how she had always pondered in her heart the visit of the shepherds at his birth; the prophecy of old Simeon that a sword would pierce her soul; the coming of the wise men who had followed the star bringing their gifts; the time of refuge in Egypt; the return from Egypt to Nazareth and their home there; the journey from Nazareth to Jerusalem when he was twelve and was lost and found in the temple; those hidden years in which Joseph died and he grew into manhood; his leaving home after his baptism by Elizabeth's son John, to wander about the countryside with his twelve disciples, followed by crowds; finally the opposition and hostility of the priests which brought him to the cross.

As the Blessed Virgin Mary stood by the cross watching her son die, she would have remembered all these events which have been revealed to us in the four Gospels.

There is the record of an incident in one of the apocryphal gospels that it was Mary who persuaded Jesus to go to the River Jordan where Elizabeth's son John, was baptising. We do know that she persuaded him to act when the supply of wine failed at the wedding at Cana.

During my visit to Israel, we passed through Cana after we had left Nazareth, on our way to the Sea of Galilee. Today Cana is called Kaifr Kana. Villagers still draw water from its well, which was the source of the water with which the servants filled the six water pots at the wedding attended by Jesus and some of his disciples.

As Mary stood by the cross she would have recalled her son's wonderful works of love after his rejection at Nazareth when he read Isaiah's prophecy of the Messiah and claimed to be the fulfilment of it.

These works were centred around the home of Simon Peter in Capernaum where Jesus had healed Peter's wife's mother.

We were shown the site of the house in Capernaum and also the ruin of a synagogue. The Roman Centurion, whose faith Jesus praised and whose servant he healed, had built a synagogue in Capernaeum, but the ruined synagogue we saw, had been built some hundreds of years later. Nevertheless it marked the site of the synagogue in which Jesus had worshipped.

Nothing else remains today of the thriving town which became the headquarters of the Galilean ministry of Jesus on the shore of Lake Galilee.

Our guide pointed out to us that Capernaeum was one of the towns whose faithlessness dismayed Jesus. The others were Bethsaida and Chorazin.

As Mary stood by the cross on that awful hill outside the walls of Jerusalem, how she must have yearned for the cool waters of the Sea of Galilee.

I shall never forget the day I spent at the Sea of Galilee. It began with a swim at 5.30 a.m. which enabled me to see the glory of the sun rising over the Galilean hills. Later we crossed the lake on a ferry in the company of some American pilgrims. As we glided over the exceedingly calm waters, a guide pointed to the various locations. It was easy to see how Jesus could have a fishing boat 'thrust out a little from the land' so that he might use it as a pulpit to address the crowds on the shore.

Before we set out on our short voyage over the lake, we had seen a fishing boat which had been in use when Jesus called Peter and his brother Andrew, and James and John to become fishers of men.

We had been staying at the Kibbutz Genossa and were told how this boat had been found.

Less rain than usual had fallen on Mount Hermon and the hills surrounding the Sea of Galilee in 1985. Consequently the level of the lake had fallen. In January 1986 two brothers who were living in the kibbutz noticed the form of a boat in the shallow water not far from Magdal, the town of Mary Magdalene. They reported their discovery to the Antiquities Department. With great care the boat was examined and taken from the seabed. It was verified that the vessel was about two thousand years old, and was typical of the boats used by the fishermen from whom Jesus chose his apostles.

A few weeks before my visit to Israel, I had seen the flagship of the Fleet of King Henry VIII, *The Mary Rose*, which had been resurrected near Portsmouth in England. The great hulk of the 450 year old ship was in a huge shelter at Portsmouth and was being constantly sprayed with fresh water. The much older and much smaller boat at Galilee was kept submerged in a clear preservative tank of water at the Kibbutz Genossa.

The other remnants of the day of Christ, apart from the steadfast hills and the shore line around the Sea of Galilee were decayed ruins, but this fishing boat 27 feet long and 7 feet wide may often have been seen and even used by Jesus or his apostles, taking the same course we were taking from Tiberias to Capernaum.

From our ferry we were shown the place of the call of the disciples. It was easy to see how, when Jesus and his disciples sailed to the quiet secluded place, the crowds followed him around the shore on foot, gathering more and more as they went, until they numbered five thousand hungry people.

'There was the place where he fed the multitude,' said the guide on our ferry, pointing to a clear place on the shore over to the port side. 'And over there was the place of the tombs where he healed the wild madman whom everyone feared, and the herd of swine ran into the sea, over that steep place.'

The engine of our boat stopped and we drifted in a silence broken occasionally by the lapping of the water.

'It was about here,' said our guide, 'that Jesus came to his disciples, walking on the water.'

One of the American tourists stepped forward with a Bible in her hand and read from Mark 6.47–51.

> And when evening came, the boat was out on the sea, and he was alone on the land. And he saw that they were making headway painfully, for the wind was against them. And about the fourth watch of the night he came to them, walking on the sea. He meant to pass by them, but when they saw him walking on the sea they thought it was a ghost, and

cried out; for they all saw him, and were terrified. But immediately he spoke to them and said, 'Take heart, it is I; have no fear.' And he got into the boat with them and the wind ceased.

Then an American pastor pointed out that often the storms and tempests of life have been used by God as a means of making his presence known. He can use the storms of sin, suffering, loneliness and despair to approach those afflicted by them, just as the tempestuous sea which caused the fear of the disciples was the means by which Jesus came to them.

The storm of anguish was raging around the Mother of Jesus as she stood by the cross, but her son used that storm to assure her of his love for her.

At the beginning of this book I referred to a conference of *The Order of St Lazarus of Jerusalem* which was held in September 1986 at Oxford.

At one of the beautiful services held in *Christ Church Cathedral Oxford*, the preacher was Bishop Kallistos Ware of *The Greek Orthodox Church*.

His theme was, *One, All and Some*. He said –

One is Holy. God is Holy. He is *the* Holy One, yet *all* are holy. Paul wrote to the saints, the holy people at Ephesus, at Corinth, at Rome. We are *all* called to be holy – yet *some* are holy, the great saints of God who have won the victory by their obedient service. Of these the Blessed Virgin Mary is the chief.

There is *one* priest, Jesus Christ our Great High Priest – yet *all* are priests. 'You are a royal priesthood – a Kingdom of priests,' wrote St Peter. Yet *some* are priests, men who derive their priesthood from the apostolic ministry, commissioned by Christ when he said, 'As my Father has sent me, so I send you.' (The apostle John standing by the cross was the representative of the priesthood of the *some*).

The Blessed Virgin Mary is the supreme example of the priesthood of all believers, offering to the Father the sacrifice of her obedient service. She became the queen of all priesthood when she said, 'Let it be to me, according to your word.'

That is why Mary *stood* at the cross. She did not fall before it in grief. She *stood* there in the attitude of her complete obedience, even though the sword prophesied by Simeon, was twisted in her own soul.

Soon Blessed Mary would understand it all, but to take care of her until then, in that moment of intense, bitter pain, her son commended her to the care of John. 'Woman, behold your son, son behold your mother.'

And as we think of them both standing by the cross, let us realise just how much greater is our revelation today than it was then, even to Mary the Mother of the Word made flesh, or to John who proclaimed that the Word was made flesh and dwelt among us, and let us pray that we may truly see Jesus as the Christ, the Son of God and that believing, we may have life in his name.

*   *   *

The terrible cry from the cross 'My God my God *why* have you forsaken me' alarmed even those who stood and mocked Jesus.

It sounded like a cry of despair, as indeed it was, because the crucifixion was so terrible.

But it was a cry of despair for the sins of mankind which made the crucifixion necessary. Jesus was truly human, and at that instant he felt the fearful weight of sin. He sank to the very lowest depths of human degredation, misery, remorse and squalor.

It would be impossible for any other person to sink lower in the mire of humanity than Jesus did at that time. He experienced the *total* weight of the evil of the world, the flesh and the devil and, with his loving heart at breaking point, he cried out, 'My God my God *why* have you forsaken me.'

He knew that his mother had not forsaken him, she had been standing there by the cross, until he had sent her away with John.

Perhaps then, Jesus remembered what we now call his Transfiguration. This was the time when he took Peter, James and John to the mountain and they saw him in radiant whiteness, talking with Moses and Elijah. They talked then, about the sacrifice he was offering at that very moment. Then the voice of his Father had reassured him, 'This is my beloved son, listen to him.'

There is some controversy about the site of the Transfiguration, whether it happened on Mount Hermon or Mount Tabor.

I like to think that it was on Mount Hermon.

The Transfiguration occurred six days after the great experience at Caesarea Philippi, when Peter had acknowledged Jesus to be the Christ, the Son of the Living God.

Mount Hermon is not far from Caesarea Philippi, but Mount Tabor is a considerable distance away.

However, what convinces me most is a verse from Psalm 133 – *the dew of Hermon shall fall on the Hill of Zion.*

From the shores of the Sea of Galilee, the mists gathering on Mount Hermon can be seen.

These mists develop into rain clouds and the winds drive them to the Hill of Zion on which Jerusalem stands. Those clouds release their moisture which falls as rain so, *the dew of Hermon falls on the Hill of Zion.*

So we think of Jesus, being transfigured on Mount Hermon, conversing there with Moses and Elijah about the sacrifice he would offer for the sins of all mankind. He came down from Mount Hermon, to ascend the Hill of Zion, there to offer his sacrifice. The experience which began on Mount Hermon was completed on the Hill of Zion.

Both Moses and Elijah had felt, as Jesus felt while he was dying on the cross, forsaken by God, but both had received the assurance of his presence and the revelation of his purpose. When the voice of the Father said, 'This is my beloved son, listen to him,' the revelation was given to the three disciples that Jesus, whom they had acknowledged to be the Christ, the Son of the living God, was indeed the fulfilment of the Law, represented by Moses and the prophets, represented by Elijah.

In his humanity Jesus felt that even his Father had forsaken him, as I suppose every one us has felt at some time in life. But we can never sink lower than Jesus on the cross. Underneath are always the everlasting arms.

But that cry of despair was actually assurance from the words of the Jewish liturgy with which Jesus was so familiar. He was beginning to recite the twenty-second psalm, which is a prophecy of the death he was dying at that time.

My God my God why have you forsaken me, why are you so far from helping me?

Our fathers trusted in you and you saved them. But why not me, I have always trusted in you.

They are mocking me, save me Lord.

They stare at me, they part my garments.

They pierced my hands and feet – I can count all my bones.

But the psalm ends with the assurance of God's presence and victory.

Praise the Lord for he has not despised the poor man in his misery, he did not hide his face from him, but heard him when he cried.

He has saved my life for himself and I shall always serve Him.

The agonised cry from the cross becomes the shout of assurance that God will never forsake those who trust him, but is with them in every situation to lift them up to victory.

As Jesus grew from infancy into boyhood in the

home at Nazareth he would have learned the psalms from Joseph and Mary.

It is easy to imagine his mother listening to him recite the psalms, the ancient songs of his people Israel, so that by the time he was twelve he would be able to stand with Joseph and sing with him in the congregation of the synagogue at Nazareth.

During those three days when as a boy of twelve he was with the learned men in the temple, we might wonder what questions he asked them.

We only know that they were questions about his Father's business. Among those questions, did he ask those teachers of the Scriptures, the meaning of this psalm, so that even as he was dying on the cross he knew that he was still about his Father's business?

The agonised cry of our Lord for the satisfaction of a human need 'I thirst,' comes very soon after the loud cry, – 'My God – my God – why have you forsaken me?' It may be said that it marks the very climax of his physical sufferings, because it is so human. The Romans always said that the worst agony of those who were crucified was the terrible torment of thirst, every vein and every artery of the whole body crying for moisture. Our Lord's cry – 'I thirst,' no matter what deeper meanings we may see in it, was primarily brought about by the feverish thirst of crucifixion.

An unknown person took a sponge and raised it on a spear to his lips. He was the last person to minister to our Lord in his life.

What a privilege that man had. His service to the dying Saviour reminds us of his own words in the twenty-fifth chapter of *St Matthew's Gospel*:

But when the Son of Man shall come in his glory, before him shall all the nations be gathered and he shall separate them as a shepherd divides the sheep from the goats.

Then shall the King say to them on his right hand, 'Come blessed of my Father, inherit the kingdom prepared for you from the foundation of the earth – for I was hungry and you gave me food, I was thirsty and you gave me drink, I was a stranger and you took me in, I was sick and you visited me, I was in prison and you came to me. Inasmuch as you have done it to one of the least of these you have done it to me.'

We may well think that the unknown person who gave Jesus a drink was privileged indeed, but our Lord has told us clearly that whatever service we render to anyone in need is service to him, and that each of us can just as surely quench his thirst today as that person did as he died on the cross.

However, although we may see in his thirst what we should do for him today, we must try to understand in his thirst on the cross what he has done for us.

He thirsted upon the cross, the natural thirst of a man dying in the heat, in order that he might give to us all, the drink which would quench all spiritual thirst, He said, 'This is my blood of the new convenant which is shed for you and for many for the forgiveness of sins. Do this as often as you drink it in memory of me.'

The thirst of Jesus was quenched for the first time in his life in the stable of Bethlehem from the breast of his blessed mother Mary.

It was quenched for the last time shortly before his death on the cross.

His first infant cry in the stable of Bethlehem was induced by his thirst, for God had become man.

The human cry of Jesus in his dying agony for the relief of a human need — 'I thirst' reveals to us the tremendous love of God who for us men and for our salvation came down from heaven.

This fact is celebrated at Christmas. St Paul, in his *Epistle to the Philippians* emphasises the great humility with which Christ came among us.

> Have this mind in you, which was also in Christ Jesus, who being in the form of God, counted it not a prize to be on an equality with God, but emptied himself, taking upon him the form of a servant, being made in the likeness of men, and being found in fashion as a man, he humbled himself and becme obedient to death, even the death of the cross (Philippians 2.5–8).

In this one sentence, St Paul bridges the gap between Christmas Day and Good Friday.

He emptied himself — he laid aside all the advantage of his heavenly glory. That is what happened at Christmas. He became obedient to death — even the death of the cross. That is what happened on Good Friday.

The Word became flesh to save man. This was the work he had come to do. This was the business of his Father which he discussed with the teachers in the temple when he was twelve and, from the cross he acknowledged that his work was complete.

The sixth utterance, 'It is finished,' is the cry of triumph – the shout of accomplishment. Like an artist putting the final brush mark on his picture, or the scientist who after years of research and study finally discovers the cure for a terrible disease. 'It is finished' is not a dying gasp of 'it's all over' – but a triumphant shout. He said himself, 'I come to do your will O God.'

At his birth we are told of the great joy of the angels who sang their prophetic hymn, 'Glory to God in the Highest and in earth peace, goodwill towards men.' This means the making of the will of man at one with the will of God.

When our Lord prayed to his Father before his death, he said, 'I have finished the work you gave me to do' (John 17.4).

The completion of the work of Christ marks the beginning of the work of the Church.

Our Lord expressed his vision of the Church as the body through which his works would be continued.

'He who believes in me will do the works that I do, and greater works than these, because I go to the Father' (John 14.12).

His works were works of healing and teaching.

The last thing I did before I finished my pilgrimage to the Holy Land was to celebrate the Eucharist in *St George's Anglican Cathedral* in Jerusalem. St George's Cathedral is of white stone, built on the lines of a typically English Gothic church.

It stands as a testimony to the acceptance by the Church of its vocation to make the teaching work of Christ greater. The present Anglican Bishop of Jerusalem, Samir Kafity, traces his Christian ancestry back to the early days of Christianity when the forefathers of the English missionaries who built the Cathedral were worshipping heathen gods in Britain, painted with woad.

Today *St George's Cathedral* is at the centre of a thriving school for children in Jerusalem. It is also the centre of *St George's College*. Christian men and women from all denominations and all races and countries come to *St George's College* for special Biblical courses.

The products of those who went out from Jerusalem into all the world, return to Jerusalem, that they too may go back into the world of their own environment and continue the work of Christ.

I was impressed by the vast representation of men and women from so many countries and churches at *St George's College*.

The work of Christ in his earthly body was completed on the cross. Now we, as living members of the body which is the extension of his incarnate life, the Church, have been charged to continue to do his works of healing and teaching, in the power of his Holy Spirit.

*   *   *

'Father into your hands I commend my spirit' is the final 'word' from the cross.

The first recorded utterance of Jesus was, 'Didn't you know that I must be about my Father's business?'

He spent the whole of his life about his Father's

business, and then, as the shadow of death folded around him, he placed himself in his Father's hands saying 'Father into your hands I commend my spirit.'

The whole purpose of his incarnate life was to glorify the Father. In his prayer to his Father recorded in the seventeenth chapter of St John's Gospel Jesus said. 'I have glorified you on earth, I have finished the work you gave me to do.' He glorified the Father by reconciling us to him, so that we might become the children of the Father.

Jesus died, certain of the presence of his Father. He shouted to the whole world his cry of triumph – 'It is finished' and then he spoke intimately to his Father, 'Father into your hands I commend my spirit.'

A representative of the world heard what he said and saw him die. When the centurion who stood by saw that he so gave up his spirit, he said, 'Truly this man was the Son of God' (Mark 15.39).

The Incarnation began when Mary said to the Father, 'into your hands I commend my body,' and it was fulfilled when the son she bore said, 'Father into your hands I commend my spirit.'

CHAPTER FOUR

The Experience of the Glory

(The Glorious Mysteries)

The first glorious mystery is the Resurrection.

> *Come see the place where Jesus lay,*
> *And hear Angelic watchers say,*
> *'He lives, Who once was slain:*
> *Why seek the living 'midst the dead?*
> *Remember how the Saviour said*
> *That He would rise again.'*

Christianity is the religion of life. The Resurrection followed the death of Christ.

We have seen that in the joyful mysteries, the role of Mary was an active one, a subjective one, it was she who was the doer.

In the sorrowful mysteries, Mary was merely a witness of the terrible events around her, over which she had no control.

In the glorious mysteries, as the representative of every one who would try to fulfil the will of God, Mary's role was objective. She, like us, was the recipient of God's acts in his Son Jesus Christ.

While the Church commemorates the death of Jesus on Good Friday, there is throughout the liturgical worship, the anticipation of the celebration of the Resurrection on Easter Day.

On Good Friday we pray:

'Almighty Father, look graciously upon this your family for which our Lord Jesus Christ was willing to be betrayed and given up into the hands of wicked men and to suffer death upon the cross, who now lives and reigns with you and the Holy Spirit, one God for ever and ever.'

The Resurrection is the first of the glorious mysteries, and it is indeed the greatest of the mysteries, upon which the significance of all the other mysteries, the joyful, the sorrowful and the glorious depends.

The fact that Jesus Christ rose from the dead is the very key of the teaching of the Church. It is the only reason why the Church exists. St Paul wrote in *The First Epistle to the Corinthians*, 'If Christ did not rise from the dead then is our preaching vain and your faith in vain.'

Only the Resurrection of Jesus could give substance to the promise of the Angel Gabriel to Mary that the Lord God would give her son the throne of his father David, and that he would reign over the house of Jacob forever and of his kingdom there would be no end.

When Mary heard the message of the Angel, her first thought was the present, 'How shall this be, I do not know a man?'

She did not question the endurance of the reign of

the Messiah for ever. At the Annunciation her question was how would it all begin.

It began through the power of the Holy Spirit, as the Church was to begin through the power of the Holy Spirit.

When Peter preached the first sermon of the Church on the day of Pentecost, he proclaimed that although the Jewish rulers had put Jesus to death, it was not possible for him to be held by death.

In *Preaching through the Christian Year 2*, Canon Frank Colquhoun called this a *Glorious Impossibility*.

There is no doubt about the reality of the death of Jesus, because there can be no doubt about the reality of his manhood. He became truly man and was subject to all of the limitations of humanity, including death.

It was not possible for death to hold Jesus because death is the separation from God which is the penalty of sin, and he was sinless. He died, because he had completely identified himself with sinful man. On the cross he paid the penalty for sin, by death.

The cross was the victory of Jesus. His Resurrection revealed what the cross already was. Therefore it was not possible for death to hold Jesus, because he had destroyed all the power of death.

In Jerusalem it was often said by those who identified the sites of incidents in the life of Jesus Christ, that Christians worship the living God rather than places. However, events are associated with places, and from places we can learn about God's handiwork. 'The Heavens declare the glory of God and the earth shows his handiwork,' wrote the psalmist. God is in every place, yet he has always used places to reveal his presence and purpose. We remember Jacob's utterance as he woke from his dream of the ladder, 'Surely the Lord is in this place and I knew it not.' Moses was made aware of God's presence in the burning bush and Isaiah had the vision of God's glory in the temple at Jerusalem.

Having laid the dead body of the crucified Saviour in a tomb as prominent as that provided by Joseph of Arimathaea, it would have been impossible for anyone to have stolen it, and very easy for the authorities to have produced it. It has been stated that the Roman emperor Hadrian, the wall builder, had attempted to obliterate the sites which were sacred to the Christians by walling them in and erecting pagan temples on them, but in doing this, he had actually preserved and identified them for the future. The mother of the emperor Constantine, Helena, was a devout Christian. When she made a pilgrimage to Jerusalem, she initiated the demolition of the pagan temples and the unearthing of the sacred places where Jesus was born, where he was crucified and where he was buried.

Constantine built a church on the site of the empty tomb in 326. This was destroyed by the Persians in 614. Later another church was built there by the Abbot Modestos. The destruction of this building in 1009 by the Khalif Hakem was the direct cause of the Crusades. The present church was built by the Crusaders and in spite of additions, fires and restorations, it has stood as the witness of the empty tomb and the Resurrection of Christ since then.

The Church of the Holy Sepulchre, better described as *The Church of the Resurrection* is actually a collection of chapels surrounding the circular church with the empty tomb in the centre of it.

Today the church is administered by three major owners and three minor owners.

The major owners are the Roman Catholic, the Greek Orthodox and the Armenian Christians. The minor owners are the Copts, the Syrians and the Abyssinians.

Having followed *The Way of the Cross*, one comes to a gate in a wall. Through the gate is a courtyard paved in stone, worn smooth by the feet of pilgrims. On the other side of the courtyard there is the entrance to *The Church of the Resurrection*.

Strangely the doors of the Church have been guarded by Moslems ever since this task was entrusted to them by Suleiman in the sixteenth century because the Christians could not agree on who should do so.

One of the leading theologians of the Anglican Church in Australia, Gilbert Sinden SSM, was attached to St George's College in Jerusalem at the time of my visit. He kindly offered to take me and some of my friends through *The Church of the Resurrection*.

During his time in Jerusalem he had grown to love every stone in the building, and was well known to all who were associated with it.

He pointed out and explained every point of the mysterious building, leading us through its dark passages by the light of his torch.

Many of the incidents surrounding the death of Jesus are identified by chapels.

We descended into one gloomy chapel which Brother Gilbert said marked the site of the prison where our Lord was held at the end of *The Via Dolorosa*, while the final preparations for the crucifixion were made.

While we were there a woman came in and bowed low before the altar, on which was a rather shabby icon of the Blessed Virgin Mary. The eyes of our Lady in the picture were closed. Later Brother Gilbert explained the reason for the woman's profound devotion.

Not long before, one of the Moslem guards making his nightly round before locking the church, had entered this chapel of Christ's prison. He looked at the icon of the Blessed Virgin. He was startled by the fact that the eyes of the Virgin were open!

The guard reported his experience, and since then other people had had a similar experience of seeing the eyes of the Virgin open.

'The Moslems love our Lady,' said Brother Gilbert.

When I looked at the icon, the eyes were closed. It was a very old and battered picture. The paint was peeling. However perhaps, if the Moslems love our Lady, the experience of the guard may have been a sign that she can indeed be a source of unity, directing people to her son, looking upon the world in love.

In another part of the church, a Roman Catholic mass was in progress. Suddenly a loud, raucous jarring bell began to ring, clanging and clanging through the whole building.

'That's the Armenians getting ready for their service,' said Brother Gilbert.

The bell stopped and then the Armenians appeared. Several were happy looking teenage boys, one extremely fat. They formed a procession, carrying candles, incense, and a banner in front of a richly robed priest. They were all singing very loudly and heartily. Then another youth who had been left behind came running along the stone pavement, grinning broadly. He was carrying the processional cross and should have been leading the procession! The others made way for him smiling happily as they went on their way to their chapel singing their introit of praise.

'That is typical of the joy these people find in their religion,' said Gilbert.

Then he told us about the way the Eastern churches celebrate the Resurrection in that ancient building. I asked him to write it all out for me. He wrote it as follows:

'On Orthodox Easter eve, when it seems that all of Christian Jerusalem is gathered in the great Church of the Resurrection (or Holy Sepulchre, as the tourists will call it), the Greek Orthodox Patriarch of Jerusalem goes into the tomb building which stands on the spot where Joseph of Arimathea's tomb received (and lost!) the body of the crucified Lord, around one o'clock in the afternoon. There is a great and sudden silence among the thousands of expectant worshippers until the glimmer of light is seen and we know that the Holy Fire has come again to assure us of the agelong truth: "Christ is risen!" Within seconds, great bundles of lighted candles are handed out from the tomb and the light is passed from Christian to Christian. Each one greets the others saying, "Christ is risen!" and the reply "Indeed he is risen!"

Some youngsters with lanterns carry the New Fire to waiting taxis, thence to all the parish churches of the country, and even by plane to Cairo, Athens and Constantinople.

Meanwhile within the great church, there is a race in progress. Greek and Armenian altar boys each take the new fire as fast as they can to their respective altars to light the altar candles. Each group tries to beat the other.

It seems that the Greek boys have an easy task. Their altar is not so far away, and on the same level as the tomb building. The Armenian boys have to climb two quite formidable flights of stairs to get to their chapel. But the Greek pilgrims bunched together, impede their acolytes, while the Armenian community clears the way and does everything possible to assist their representatives.

If, as usually happens, the end result is an Armenian "victory" one of the Armenian bishops or priests climbs precariously out onto a ledge on the inside of the great rotunda around the tomb and waves a bundle of lighted candles in delighted jubilation.

So the great joy of the Resurrection of Jesus becomes part of our simpler and more direct human joys, for this is nothing less than simple and pure hearts taking that joy into their daily life.'

Brother Gilbert's faith and intellect certainly enabled him to find in *The Church of the Resurrection* a very wonderful means of proclaiming the truth of the risen Saviour. I know he still believes that, in that part of the earth, the greatest act in the handiwork of God for the salvation of man is continually being shown forth to the world as pilgrims behold the empty tomb and the place where the body of Christ was laid.

The tomb is identified by a small cell lined with marble. Only two or three people can enter at the same time. Oil lamps belonging to the various churches hang before the stone which is covered by a slab of white marble on which the dead body of Jesus was laid.

I cannot say that I was aware of the presence of Christ there in any dramatic way. It certainly was an emotional experience. I was more conscious of the promise of the risen Lord to be with his followers in every place. 'Lo, I am with you always.' This is the real meaning of Easter.

Brother Gilbert took us around to another part of the building up some steps.

'Here is the site of the crucifixion,' he said. Two chapels were there, side by side, divided by two pillars. One is a Roman Catholic Chapel called *The Chapel of the Nailing to the Cross*. The other is an Orthodox chapel called *The Chapel of the Raising of the Cross*.

With other pilgrims we approached the altar in *The Chapel of the Raising of the Cross*. A Greek priest was replacing some of the many candles which are kept alight constantly.

Each pilgrim in turn knelt silently before the altar and placed his or her hands into a hole under it, surrounded by a silver edge, to touch the place where the cross had been placed.

What prayer could one say other than – 'O Saviour of the World, who by Thy Cross and Precious Blood has redeemed us, Save us and help us we humbly beseech Thee O Lord.'

The chapel on the other side, *The Chapel of the Nailing to the Cross*, also marks the place where the mother of Jesus held his lifeless body in her arms after it had been taken down from the cross to be prepared for burial in the tomb. The place where Mary held the body of her son is designated by a marble slab. It is a beautiful thought, that she who held the body of God's son in her arms at his birth, should have done so on the completion of his work on earth, as the final sign of her own supreme obedience.

After that timeless experience on the site of the crucifixion, we descended the steps to another chapel which Brother Gilbert called *The Chapel of Adam.* Here he pointed out a large rock behind a glass facing in the wall of the chapel. Above this wall was the area from which we had just descended, containing *The Chapel of the Raising of the Cross.* The rock behind the glass was directly below the altar before which I had knelt and touched the silver rimmed hole. There was a large crack in the rock, from the top to the bottom.

Sometimes it is necessary to distinguish between spiritual truth and factual truth.

Our Lord told his parable, *The Good Samaritan.*It contains spiritual truth, but we do not really know if the story is factually true.

So the Genesis story of the disobedience of Adam and Eve contains spiritual truth. Man, using his freewill, disobeyed God and sinned. Because man sinned, he was separated from God.

Adam and Eve, the representatives of humanity were driven out of the Garden of Eden. Eventually they died and, according to the tradition, they were buried beneath the hill of Calvary, in the place identified by *The Chapel of Adam.*

This tradition proclaims a great spiritual truth.

According to the tradition, when the earthquake occurred at the death of Jesus, the rock behind the glass was rent, enabling the blood of Christ to flow through it on to the graves of Adam and Eve.

St Matthew records that when Jesus died, the dead arose (Matthew 27.51–53), and the tradition states that the first of the dead to rise were Adam and Eve. Adam means *man* and Eve means *life*. In the Genesis story, Adam and Eve are the representatives of humanity rebelling against God. So the tradition proclaims the truth stated by St Paul. 'As in Adam all die, so through Christ shall all be made alive.' (1 Corinthians 15.22). The *all* includes Adam and Eve.

I must admit that, when I stood in *The Chapel of Adam*, gazing at the cracked rock, and heard Brother Gilbert tell me about the tradition, I was overcome by the reality of its great proclamation.

Here indeed was the stark and vivid declaration of the Christian Gospel.

St Peter wrote that after the death of Jesus, in the spirit which had departed from his crucified body, he preached to the dead (1 Peter 3.19; 4.6).

The purpose of his preaching was to enable all who had lived before him, to accept the benefit of his sacrifice for the sins of the whole world. Consequently *the dead*, led by Adam and Eve rose to life.

According to the Genesis story it was the dis-obedience of Adam which caused death, and so in Adam all must die. For since by man, Adam, came death even so in Christ shall all be made alive.

The dead who rose up after the death of Christ were seen, but only for a time, for they, having been redeemed by the blood of Christ went on to the fulfilment of their humanity into the place which had been prepared for them in the house of the Lord, by Christ himself (John 14.2).

The Resurrection of Jesus means for us that, while death is an inevitable part of humanity, it has no power to separate us from God, because it will be merely an incident in life as we proceed to the achievement of our eternal destiny, to inherit the Kingdom of Heaven.

The service of *Holy Baptism* links each one of us with the Resurrection of Christ because Baptism represents a death to the sinful nature of humanity, its burial in the water and the resurrection to new life. Through Baptism we become children of the risen life.

We often fail to grasp the beauty of this fact when we see a baby baptised. The child becomes a child of the Resurrection.

St Paul exhorts us in his letter to the Colossians – 'If you are risen with Christ, seek those things which are above.'

There is a pious belief that our Lord appeared to his mother soon after he had risen from the dead.

In some ways it seems natural that he should have done so, but actually there would have been no need.

His appearances to the others were to strengthen their faith and to commission them for the work ahead. Mary's faith needed no strengthening. Thirty three years before, she had received her commission, and had always been faithful to her response, 'I am the handmaid of the Lord, let it be to me, according to your word.'

Perhaps there was significance in the words of Jesus to Thomas. 'Because you have seen you have believed, blessed are those who have not seen and yet have believed.' Did not Mary herself say that all generations would call her blessed?

Any appearance of the risen Lord to Mary would have come after her belief that he had risen.

＊　　　　＊　　　　＊

The second glorious mystery is the Ascension.

> *The holy apostolic band*
> *Upon the Mount of Olives stand,*
> *And with the Virgin-mother see*
> *Jesu's resplendent majesty.*
> *To whom the Angels, drawing nigh,*
> *'Why stand and gaze upon the sky?*
> *This is the Saviour!' thus they say,*
> *'This is his noble triumph-day!'*

He was lifted up, and a cloud received him out of their sight.

The old English word for lift up was *heave*. The past tense was not heaved, but *heaven*.

It is important to understand that when St Luke wrote in *The Acts of the Apostles* that Jesus was *heaven*, and a cloud received him out of their sight, he was proclaiming a spiritual truth. To the Jews, the cloud was always the symbol of God's presence and his glory. The presence of God was seen as a pillar of cloud by day and fire by night, going before the Israelites when they fled from Egypt and, through the wilderness entered the Promised Land.

When Moses went up to Mount Sinai to receive the

Ten Commandments, God called him and said, 'I come to you in a thick cloud, that the people may hear when I speak with you and believe you forever.'

It is quite clear that Mary, the Mother of Jesus, was amongst those who witnessed and understood the spiritual meaning of the Ascension, that her son had returned, in his human body, to the glory which he had laid aside at his birth.

The last actual biblical reference to her is in the first chapter of *The Acts of the Apostles*. Here it is recorded that Mary was with the company of believers who came to the upper room after witnessing the Ascension, and who remained together in prayer and supplication. During this period of ten days, they chose Matthias to take the place of Judas, and waited for the outpouring of the Holy Spirit.

St Luke, at the conclusion of his Gospel emphasises that there was no sense of parting at the Ascension but great joy. The company of believers, including Mary, returned to Jerusalem with great joy and were continually in the temple, praising and blessing God.

What was begun in the womb of the Blessed Virgin Mary was completed at the Ascension. Through the body of Mary, Christ took our humanity. The Word became flesh and dwelt amongst us. He did not cease to be God, but he laid aside the advantage of being God.

In that human body which Mary gave him, Jesus ascended into Heaven as God and man. He came to earth as God and also became man, and as God and man he ascended, triumphant over the death he had died on the cross, through his resurrection from it.

It has been said that the believers were intensely conscious of the presence of Jesus after the Ascension, because he had ascended out of the sight of a few, that he might dwell in the hearts of all, out of the here, into the everywhere.

The Ascension took place on the Mount of Olives, above the Garden of Gethsemane towards Bethany which lies on its eastern side.

The Mount of Olives rises to a bare rock ridge, from the Kedron Valley which separates it from Jerusalem's east wall. On the slopes of the Mount of Olives there are the graves of many Jews. On the other side of the Kedron valley on the slope down from the eastern wall, are thousands of Moslem tombs. The grave stones are gleaming white. Perhaps our Lord chose to ascend from the Mount of Olives because of the belief, now also shared by the Moslems, that the Last Judgement would be held in the Kedron Valley between Jerusalem and the Mount of Olives.

The view from the top of the Mount of Olives reveals all the parched ruggedness of the Judean highlands. Many have likened to the surface of the moon, the barren hills, the Mountains of Moab, which seem to be tumbling over each other as they descend to the Dead Sea from 3000 feet above sea level to 1200 feet below sea level.

Jesus knew this view well. Perhaps he saw it as symbolic of the hardness of the hearts of Jerusalem's inhabitants when he wept over the city, before he entered it in triumph and the people wanted to make him their king. The Golden Gate, which is the site of that triumphal entry has been walled up for centuries.

The Golden Gate of Jerusalem may now be walled up, but by his Ascension, Jesus Christ has opened the gate of the Kingdom of Heaven to all believers.

Our Lord had told his followers to wait for the outpouring of the Holy Spirit who was to lead them to all truth. The Holy Spirit would unfold to them the work of Jesus in Heaven as the Great High Priest, eternally offering to the Father the sacrifice he had made for the sins of the world.

Taught by the Holy Spirit, they were to learn and go out to teach the deepest significance of the Holy Eucharist, as the fulfilment of the imperfect sacrifices of the old covenant.

In *The Epistle to the Hebrews* we are shown that our Lord's work as the Great High Priest in Heaven is the completion of that foreshadowing of his perfect offering by the sacrifices of the old covenant.

The Ascension of Jesus was seen to correspond to the High Priest's entry into the Holy of Holies in the temple, there to make the oblation of the victim's blood.

The Eucharist is always to bridge the interval of time which separates man from Calvary and so enable him to ascend in heart and mind to union with the great High Priest in Heaven.

The High Priest of the old covenant took the blood of the sacrificial victim through the veil in the temple which concealed the sanctuary, the holiest part, from the view of the people. This veil was torn during the earthquake at the crucifixion (Matthew 27.51).

Behind the veil, the priest offered the blood to God, on behalf of those for whom the sacrifice was made, sprinkling it around the Mercy Seat on the Ark of the Covenant, which represented the presence of God.

As our Great High Priest, the risen Lord ascended into Heaven, veiled from the sight of man. Before the throne of his Father in the timelessness of Heaven, he offers his own blood and pleads the sacrifice of his crucified humanity for all mankind, in every age.

The Blood of Christ is concerned with the sacrificial work of the *risen* Lord. It is evidence of what Jesus Christ does for us in his resurrection life. He shed blood that we might share in his risen life.

There is one sacrifice, one priest and one altar. Because the Eucharist is the solemn memorial of the sacrifice of Christ which he made on the altar of the cross, and also because it is the ever present sign of his timeless priestly activity in Heaven, the table on which it is celebrated is called an altar. The living agent, ordained to represent him in setting apart the bread and wine to be his body and blood, derives his priesthood from the Great High Priest himself, as he acts for the whole Church in its priestly character.

On the altar, wherever the Eucharist is celebrated, the great love of God is revealed. The Great High Priest renews us by our union with him and makes us partakers of his own sacrifice.

The pain which the Blessed Virgin Mary experienced was all part of that sacrifice because her suffering would have added to his own suffering. He revealed this in his tenderness to her when he commended her to the care of his beloved disciple John.

*   *   *

The third glorious mystery is the outpouring of the Holy Spirit.

At the third hour a rushing noise
Came like the tempest's sudden voice,
And mingled with the Apostles' prayer,
Proclaiming loud that God was there.
On each the fire, descending, stood
In quivering tongues' similitude –
Tongues, that their words might ready prove,
And fire, to make them flame with love.

The Blessed Virgin Mary with the company of believers, would have witnessed the signs of the Holy Spirit on the day of Pentecost, ten days after the Ascension of Jesus into Heaven.

> When the day of Pentecost came, they were all together in one place. Suddenly a sound like the blowing of a violent wind came from heaven and filled the whole house where they were sitting. They saw what seemed to be tongues of fire that separated and came to rest on each of them. All of them were filled with the Holy Spirit and began to speak in other tongues as the Spirit enabled them. (Acts 2. 1–4).

This outpouring took place in the room in which the Last Supper was held. In the same room the risen Christ appeared to his apostles and commissioned them with the authority he had received from his Father. The room is known as *The Coenaculum* which means a dining hall.

It is said that the followers of Christ, in the formative years of the Church, venerated this place above any of the other places associated with Jesus. It was the site of the fulfilment of his birth in Bethlehem, his baptism in the Jordan, his transfiguration on Mount

Hermon, his death on Calvary, his resurrection from the tomb of Joseph of Arimathaea and his ascension from the Mount of Olives.

'Wait in Jerusalem and you shall receive power from on high, the promise of my Father,' he had said.

That promise was fulfilled in *The Coenaculum*.

The presence of the Holy Spirit was made known by the appearance of tongues of fire and the enabling of the disciples to speak of the wonderful works of God in different languages.

This event marked the beginning of the work of the Church as the extension of the incarnate life of Christ.

Before Jesus was born, the Holy Spirit spoke to man through the prophets of *The Old Testament*. Mary of Nazareth was called to become the mother of the Messiah whom the prophets, inspired by the Holy Spirit, said would come. When she asked the angelic messenger how she could conceive a child without contact with a man, the angel replied, 'the Holy Ghost will come upon you and the power of the Highest will overshadow you' (Luke 1.35).

Through the power of the Holy Spirit, although she was a virgin, Mary was enabled to do what seemed impossible, conceive and bear a son. So the Holy Spirit of God will enable every one of us to do whatever God wants us to do, no matter how impossible it may seem, if we desire to do what God wills.

But it may be asked, 'If the Holy Spirit had always been active in human life before Jesus was born, what was the significance of his spectacular coming to the apostles at Pentecost?'

Before Jesus came into the world, the nature of

God was gradually revealed to man through the prophets. In the human life of Jesus the glory of God was fully revealed.

The Holy Spirit, who came down at Pentecost, fulfilling the promise of Jesus, certainly had always been active in man, but at Pentecost he was made known to man in a new and more definite character. He was made known as the Spirit of the risen, glorified Christ, triumphant over sin and death.

Jesus himself received the Holy Spirit in his humanity when he was baptised by John the Baptist. In the power of the Holy Spirit he carried out his ministry. What he received being man, he gives to man because he is also divine.

When the Holy Spirit came to the followers of Jesus at Pentecost, they felt the exhilaration of being filled with the same power which had been in Jesus and which for ever after, was never to be separated from Jesus.

The Acts of the Apostles and *The Epistles* testify how those who believed in Jesus Christ were mightily aware of the Holy Spirit within them as an ever present force. As it was glorious then for the followers of Christ to live with such a sense of divine energy, so it should be glorious for us today.

What Jesus promised would be done by the Holy Spirit in and for his apostles, he intended to be done by the same Spirit in and for every believer, until his coming again in glory.

*　　　*　　　*

The fourth glorious mystery is the Assumption of Mary into Heaven.

> *Heaven with transcendent joys her entrance graced,*
> *Next to his throne her Son his Mother placed;*
> *And here below, now she's of heaven possest,*
> *All generations are to call her blest.*

The Blessed Virgin Mary is the example of obedience for us all. She submitted herself to the will of God and was promised the power of the Holy Spirit to enable her to do whatever God required of her.

If we submit ourselves to God's will, we too shall receive the same enabling power. Such submission will certainly bring joy, and it may bring pain as it did for Mary, but it will certainly lead to glory.

She whom the angel called *the highly favoured of God*; she whom her cousin Elizabeth said was *blessed among women*; she who called herself *the handmaid of the Lord* and faithfully did his will, would certainly be assured of her place in the endless kingdom of her son which had been promised by the angel.

It has been stressed that the Rosary is not an act of worship directed to the Blessed Virgin Mary, but is actually a meditation on the statement of Jesus in the sixteenth verse of the third chapter of *St John's Gospel*, 'God so loved the world, that he gave his only begotten son, that whoever believes in him should not perish but have everlasting life.'

The Rosary is a meditation on the love of God revealed in Jesus, and on God's ultimate plan for all who are willing to accept his love.

The fourth glorious mystery, the Assumption of the

Blessed Virgin Mary into Heaven, shows us the completion of God's plan, because what happened at the
end of her earthly life is what is promised at the end of
the earthly life of all believers. They shall pass from
death to life.

The word *assumption* was originally applied to the
death of any saint. Many saints are commemorated on
the day of their death. It seems logical therefore that the
passing of the Blessed Virgin Mary from this world
should be commemorated.

As she shared her son's earthly pain, so now she is
the sharer of his glory.

The promise of Jesus is for his mother and it is the
same for us all. Mary fulfilled her vocation, but she
knew that just as Jesus himself in his humanity, had no
advantage over anyone else, neither would she, as his
mother, have any advantage. When Jesus said, 'Whoever does the will of my Father is my brother, my sister
and my mother,' he was not belittling his mother, but
he was raising all who do the will of his Father to the
same status as his mother.

'In my Father's house are many rooms,' said Jesus,
'if it were not so, would I have told you that I go to
prepare a place for you, that where I am, there you may
be also?' (John 14.3).

When his mother passed from this life, she was
received into that room or special place, which her son
had prepared for her in his Father's house, just as all
who submit themselves to God's will, shall ultimately
be received into the place prepared for them.

Mary has her own special place, not only because
she is the Mother of God Incarnate, but because of her

obedience in her unique and wonderful vocation to the will and purpose of the Heavenly Father.

*   *   *

So we come to the fifth glorious mystery, the Coronation of the Blessed Virgin Mary.

> *She suffered with her Son below,*
> *She's crowned with him above,*
> *His pain and glory she does know,*
> *The mystery of his love.*

All who have ministered to Jesus, all who have fed Jesus as Mary fed him, all who have wrapped him in swaddling clothes as Mary clothed him; all who have nursed him and comforted him as Mary did, will hear him say, 'Come blessed children of my Father, receive the Kingdom prepared for you from the beginning of the world, because I was hungry and you fed me, naked and you clothed me, thirsty and you gave me drink; whenever you did it to the least of my children, you did it to me' (Matthew 25.40).

Those who inherit a kingdom receive a crown. 'Be faithful to death and I shall give you the crown of life' (Revelation 2.10).

The Blessed Virgin Mary was faithful to death. She stood by the cross of her son. She who had witnessed the glory of his risen life and had passed from this world, enfolded by his love, most certainly would have received her crown of life.

When St Paul was in prison awaiting execution, he wrote to Timothy:

> The time of my departure is at hand, I have fought a good fight, I have finished my course, I have kept the faith, now I know there is laid up for me a crown of righteousness which the Lord the righteous judge shall give me at that day and not to me only, but to all those who love his appearing (2 Timothy 4.8).

The great promise of the Gospel is that we shall not merely be subjects of the Kingdom of God, but that we shall *reign* with Christ in glory.

These are earthly terms to describe to us wonder and glory which are indescribable.

The fifth glorious mystery, the Coronation of the Blessed Virgin Mary, points to the ultimate goal of our human destiny.

In the old preface for Ascension Day we prayed:

> 'For as we believe our Lord Jesus Christ to have ascended into Heaven so we may in heart and mind thither ascend and reign with him in glory.'

The Kingdom in which the faithful reign with Christ and for which he taught us to pray, to come on earth as it is in Heaven, is a kingdom of right relationships in which each one loves the other and desires only what is good for the other; it is a kingdom in which no laws are necessary because each person regards himself or herself as the servant of the others.

To reign with Christ in glory is to be a servant, because he came to be the servant of all. To serve in love is to know the glory of God.

The seed of that glory is sown in Baptism, in which we are made children of God, members of Christ and heirs of the Kingdom of Heaven.

The Coronation of the Blessed Virgin Mary is the coronation prepared for all who desire to be the servants of God and who can respond to God's call, 'Behold I am the handmaid, I am the servant of the Lord.'

We have seen how Mary responded to God's call, how she watched over her child who was her saviour and ours, how she pondered the mystery of his birth, and kept in her heart the holy things she pondered, how she suffered with him and shared his pain and, through his death, and resurrection, at no light cost to herself, won her crown.

It may seem incongruous to relate the Coronation of the Blessed Virgin Mary to *The Dead Sea Scrolls*, however, there are some points of common interest.

When I was in the region of the Dead Sea I was shown a cave in the barren hillside which rises from the western shore in the Qumran area. In 1947 a Bedouin boy had followed a mountain goat into this cave and there he found a strange jar containing an ancient parchment. He reported his discovery, which was proved to be some writings from what we know as *The Old Testament*. A thorough search was made of the area and in ten other caves writings from every book of *The Old Testament*, except *Esther*, were found.

These manuscripts were the work of a sect known as the Essenes, who from 100 B.C. had withdrawn from the world to that barren, hard isolated region to dedicate themselves to God and prepare to be worthy citizens of the new Jerusalem which they believed would be Heaven on Earth.

They copied the scriptures and, when the Roman Army plundered Jerusalem and ravaged the country in A.D. 70, they hid their sacred writings in the caves where they were concealed for nineteen hundred years.

Many of the Essenes perished at the hands of the Romans when they besieged Masada, not far away from Qumran.

The scrolls have been dated a thousand years earlier than any other existing manuscripts of *The Old Testament*, but the text has hardly changed in all the copying and recopying since then.

The most complete scroll is *The Book of Isaiah*.

Today *The Dead Sea Scrolls* are housed in Jerusalem in *The Shrine of the Book*. The building has been designed to represent the caves in which the scrolls were found. In the centre, beneath a white dome which represents the lid of the type of jar in which the scrolls were preserved, the 26 feet long scroll of Isaiah has been set around a large cylinder. On top of this cylinder is a huge replica of one of the scroll handles pointing upwards beneath the white dome.

The Book of Isaiah contains the most powerful prophecies in *The Old Testament* concerning the coming of the Messiah.

'A Virgin will conceive and bear a son who will be called Emanuel, God with us.' The Messiah is foretold as a King who will reign in righteousness as a Prince of Peace, and as a Priest who will offer himself as a suffering servant, to bear the sins of his people through the sacrifice of himself.

The Book of Isaiah ends with a description of Jerusalem, personified as a queen in glory, who will gather her children in peace.

I have mentioned *The Church of the Annunciation* in Nazareth with its tower which seen from the inside represents a white lily. Beneath this white lily canopy the place is identified where Mary accepted the challenge of God's angel to be the instrument through which Isaiah's prophecies were to be fulfilled.

Beneath the white canopy in *The Shrine of the Book* in Jerusalem is the scroll of Isaiah foretelling the advent of the Messiah.

Isaiah saw Jerusalem as the mother of God's children. John the Evangelist described how Mary's son commended his mother to us all through him, the disciple whom Jesus loved. 'Son – daughter, behold your mother.'

Isaiah saw Jerusalem clothed in glory and wrote, 'Arise, shine for your light has come and the glory of the Lord rises upon you. Your sons come from far, and your daughters are carried on the arm. You will be a crown of splendour in the Lord's hand.'

John, in the last book of the Bible wrote: 'A great and wondrous sign appeared in Heaven, a woman clothed with the sun, with the moon under her feet and a crown of twelve stars on her head' (Revelation 12.1).

Mary is crowned with glory because she is the mother of the King of Kings, the Sun of Righteousness whose radiance clothes her with glory. She has the moon at her feet. The moon which shines in the reflected glory of the sun which will rise on the earth, represents *The Old Testament* through which the light of the coming Sun of Righteousness shines. The crown of twelve stars identifies Mary as the one chosen out of all the tribes of Israel to be the mother of God incarnate.

Mary's crown of twelve stars is a reminder that she was chosen by God, from the people he chose to be the people through whom he would reveal his plan and purpose for the whole of creation.

The Dead Sea Scrolls were discovered early in the Atomic age, the age of materialism, the age of the fear of a nuclear holocaust. For those who have faith, the discovery can be seen as a sign from the creator of all things, including nuclear power, that he is still working his purpose out and that his words will never pass away.

The prophecies contained in the writings of *The Dead Sea Scrolls* were fulfilled in Jesus Christ. The representative of our humanity in their fulfilment was the Blessed Virgin Mary. *The Dead Sea Scrolls*, emphasise the changelessness of the written word, which points to the coming of the eternal Word which became flesh through the obedience of Mary.

Earlier in this chapter I mentioned the Moslem guard in *The Church of the Holy Sepulchre*, who saw the icon in which the eyes of the Blessed Virgin were open, in *The Chapel of Christ's Imprisonment*.

Let us open our eyes to the truth of God's word and free Christ from the imprisonment of the doubts and fears of this materialistic age. Let us read the words which Mary spoke to the servants at the wedding at Cana, and apply them to ourselves – 'Whatever he says to you, do it.'

If all who follow Christ can truly do this, and obey

as Mary obeyed, we shall solve not only the problems of the divisions of the Church, but there are enough of us to bring the Kingdom of God on earth as it is in Heaven.

Mary, on behalf of all humanity, accepted her vocation to be the mother of God's son, therefore through her obedience, each one of us has our own special share in the pain of Christ's passion and the glory of his risen and ascended life.

I conclude with a quotation from an unknown writer, which sums up very beautifully the reason why the Blessed Virgin Mary should be honoured by the Church of God.

'If I be accused of wasting on the Mother of my Lord, affections which he has jealously reserved to himself, I will appeal from the charge to his judgment, and lay the case before him at any stage of his earthly life. I will kneel before his cradle at Bethlehem, and acknowledge that, while I have worshipped him with the Shepherds, and with the Magi have presented to him oblations of gold and frankincense and myrrh, I have not scrupled to make a humbler offering of reverence to the Mother, who, in the winter frost of that unsheltered stable, went down to the Gates of the World to let him in. Or I will meet him as the Holy Family repose on their desert path to Egypt, and confess that, while I have sympathised with him in his early flight, I have not withheld my love from her whose fatigue and pain were increased a thousandfold by his. Or I will seek him in the Holy House at Nazareth, and tell him that, in loving her, I have but tried to imitate his example, who came from Heaven to be my model, as of every other virtue, so of filial affection. Or finally, I will approach a more awful tribunal, and, prostrate at the foot of his cross, I will own to him that, while I have adored his wounds and wept at his sufferings, I have not restrained my compassion for her whom I saw resignedly standing by his side, clasping to her heart the piercing sword of agony, which transfixed his own. And to the judgement of Jesus I will gladly bow, and his meek mouth shall speak my sentence, and I will not fear it. For I have already heard it spoken from his cross, to me, to you, to his whole Church, "Behold thy Mother!"'